Analogies 1

- Problem-Solving Strategies
- Exercises for Analysis
- Vocabulary Study

Arthur Liebman

Educators Publishing Service
Cambridge and Toronto

About the Author

Arthur Liebman, Ph.D., author and editor of more then a dozen books ranging on subjects from Sherlock Holmes to Shakespeare, has taught English on all levels from junior high through graduate school. A recognized expert on college preparatory material, he has conducted Scholastic Aptitude Test review classes for more then twenty years. Dr. Liebman, currently on the faculty of Adelphi University in New York, is also the creator of a number of popular electronic games.

Printed in USA

ISBN 978-0-8388-2225-8

12 13 MNG 12 11

WARM-UP 1

Directions: Select the pair of words that most nearly expresses the relationship of the pair of key words in capital letters. Circle the letter preceding the pair you choose. Write a bridge-sentence on the lines provided before selecting your answer.

1. CHAIN : METAL : :
   a. newspaper : events
   b. ribbon : cloth
   c. house : stone
   d. tie : stripes
   e. cigarette : tobacco

   Bridge Sentence: _____

   _____

2. CHEESE : CRACKERS : :
   a. spoon : fork
   b. candy : wrapper
   c. belt : pants
   d. cookie : snack
   e. butter : bread

   _____

   _____

3. CHICKEN : FEATHERS : :
   a. elephant : trunk
   b. tiger : claws
   c. fur : bear
   d. fish : scales
   e. parakeet : cage

   _____

   _____

4. HORSE : STABLE : :
   a. boat : ocean
   b. airplane : clouds
   c. diamond : ring
   d. walrus : ice
   e. car : garage

   _____

   _____

5. GATHER : TOGETHER : :
   a. scatter : apart
   b. practice : display
   c. tell : explain
   d. organize : finish
   e. discover : travel

   _____

   _____

6. GIANT : DWARF : :
   a. kind : cruel
   b. mountain : hill
   c. elf : monster
   d. child : father
   e. stream : river

   _____

   _____

7. HOOK : COAT : :
   a. shelf : book
   b. laundry : shirt
   c. mouth : gum
   d. diamond : baseball
   e. ring : round

   _____

   _____

8. CRAWL : WALK : :
   a. grow : born
   b. swim : float
   c. swallow : chew
   d. listen : agree
   e. scribble : write

   _____

   _____

9. CALF : COW : :
   a. cat : kitten
   b. woman : girl
   c. puppy : dog
   d. shower : storm
   e. path : road

   _____

   _____

10. SHOUT : LOUD : :
    a. laugh : happy
    b. sad : cry
    c. smile : friendly
    d. whisper : soft
    e. exercise : energetic

    _____

    _____

3. Problem

COLOR : PAINTING : :
a. bud : flower
b. brick : wall
c. cereal : grain
d. melody : music
e. statue : museum

Step 1: Bridge-Sentence: *Color is part of a painting.*

Sentences	Analyses
a. *A bud is part of a flower.*	No. A bud becomes a flower. It is a flower that is not in full bloom yet.
b. *A brick is part of a wall.*	This seems to work.
c. *Cereal is part of grain.*	No. Cereal is made of grain.
d. *Melody is a part of music.*	Seems correct.
e. *A statue is part of a museum.*	Not exactly. A statue may be *in* a museum, but is not *part* of the building's structure.

Both *b* and *d* seem correct, so a second step must be taken.

Step 2: Both *music* and *painting* are arts. *Brick* is not.

Answer: (d) melody : music

Now it's time to do some analogies on your own as "warm-ups" for the rest of the analogy units in this book. Each Warm-Up exercise on the following pages consists of ten analogy problems. When you finish each exercise, you will see explanations for solving the problems. Studying these explanations should help you understand any problem you found too difficult.

CONTENTS

TO THE TEACHER

Analogies 1 is a worktext designed to introduce students to analogy problem solving and to provide them with opportunities for vocabulary study.

Its three-part organization is much like that of *Analogies 2* and *Analogies 3*, the books which complete this series. However, as the introductory volume, *Analogies 1* contains more basic vocabulary, and Part 1, which presents analogies and strategies for solving them, contains more explanatory material and more exercises on this material. Both the content and the visual design of Part 1 will enlighten and reassure students who may be encountering analogies for the first time.

Part 2 contains three groups of analogies, with each group composed of one hundred items. For manageable practice, each of these groups is subdivided into five units each containing twenty items. Part 3 consists of three vocabulary groups of one hundred words each, with the defined and alphabetized words representing some of the most difficult vocabulary in the corresponding analogy group. The vocabulary entries may be studied before doing the analogies, or they may be used as independent vocabulary exercises as part of a vocabulary-building program.

Additional practice on analogy problem solving and on the vocabulary contained in the worktext is available in *Analogies 1, 6 Analogy and 6 Vocabulary Quizzes*, a booklet of perforated pages. Permission is given to reproduce these quizzes for use with *Analogies 1*.

TO THE STUDENT

This book is designed to introduce you to analogies, which are types of questions that appear on so many important standardized tests. Analogies may give you some difficulty later when you take tests like the new Scholastic Assessment Test I (SAT I) if you do not practice doing analogy problems well before such exams.

But there's no need to be too apprehensive or anxious. This book will help you relax and feel more confident about doing analogies. If you study it carefully, you will see that analogies are not as difficult as they seem to be at first. *Analogies 1* will teach you a reliable method for solving analogy problems and for avoiding the standard "traps" that appear over and over again on analogy tests.

While "practice" may not necessarily "make perfect," practice on solving analogy problems certainly will lead to greater skill and better test scores.

WHAT ARE ANALOGIES?

Analogies that appear on tests are actually problems for you to solve. Each analogy problem consists of one pair of words called *key words* followed by five other pairs of words. You must decide which of the five choices is most like the pair of key words.

Example:

Key Words
CHAIR : DESK

Choices (You must decide which pair below is most like the pair of key words.)
a. sand : beach
b. stool : piano
c. table : bench
d. chimney : house
e. grass : ground

HOW DO YOU SOLVE AN ANALOGY PROBLEM?

The best way to begin to solve an analogy problem is to make up a very simple sentence that shows the relationship between the key words. In the analogy above, your sentence could be:

You sit on a chair near a desk.

Here are some other examples of sentences that you could make up to go with key words.

Key Words	Sentences
RUG : FLOOR	*A rug covers a floor.*
PENCIL : LEAD	*A pencil contains lead.*
WEIGHTLIFTER : STRENGTH	*A weightlifter has strength.*
WISE : FOOLISH	*Wise is the opposite of foolish.*

Now that you've seen how to put the key words into a sentence, we'll continue with the original analogy problem. It is stated again below.

Problem

CHAIR : DESK : :
a. sand : beach
b. stool : piano
c. table : bench
d. chimney : house
e. grass : ground

We've already decided that our sentence for the key words will be:

You sit on a chair near a desk.

Once you've written a sentence for the key words, you apply its pattern to the five choices that follow the key words, and you analyze each sentence to see which one makes the most sense.

1

Sentences	Analyses
a. *You sit on the sand near a beach.*	No. The sand is not *near* the beach; it is *part of* the beach.
b. *You sit on a stool near a piano.*	This sounds good, but don't stop until you've "checked out" all five sentences.
c. *You sit on a table near a bench.*	No. Things are reversed here. You should be sitting on the bench, not the table.
d. *You sit on a chimney near a house.*	No. A chimney is not *near* a house; it is *attached to* a house.
e. *You sit on grass near the ground.*	No. Grass is not *near* the ground; it is *part of* the ground.

Answer: (b) stool : piano

You can tell that this is the correct answer because it is the only pair of words that fits the pattern of the sentence that you constructed for the key words.

Now let's try another analogy problem.

Problem

INSTRUCTOR : CLASS : :
a. artist : paint
b. doctor : medicine
c. scientist : facts
d. tutor : pupil
e. school : students

Our sentence for the key words could be:

An instructor teaches a class.

The next step is to use the pattern of the sentence for the key words for each of the five choices that follow the key words. As you write each sentence, analyze it to see if it makes sense.

Sentences	Analyses
a. *An artist teaches paint.*	No. This sentence does not make sense.
b. *A doctor teaches medicine.*	No. A doctor may teach *about* medicine, but he or she would be teaching people, not medicine.
c. *A scientist teaches facts.*	The things that a scientist teaches may be facts, but the scientist is not directing

	her teaching to facts, but to people.
d. *A tutor teaches a pupil.*	Sounds correct, but go through all the choices before making your final decision.
e. *A school teaches students.*	Students are taught in a school but not by the school. They are taught by teachers in a school.

Answer: (d) tutor : pupil

This is the correct answer because it fits the pattern of the sentence you made up for the key words, and TUTOR : PUPIL is more like the key words INSTRUCTOR : CLASS than any of the other choices.

And, here's a final example for this section.

Problem

SOLDIER : MILITARY : :
a. reader : interested
b. battleship : naval
c. violinist : musical
d. bookkeeper : female
e. doctor : young

Our sentence for the key words could be:

A soldier is a military person.

Sentences	**Analyses**
a. *A reader is an interested person.*	Not necessarily.
b. *A battleship is a naval person.*	A battleship is naval, but it is not a person.
c. *A violinist is a musical person.*	Sounds right but don't make a final decision before checking the remaining choices.
d. *A bookkeeper is a female person.*	Sometimes, but not always.
e. *A doctor is a young person.*	Maybe, but not necessarily.

Answer: (c) violinist : musical

This answer is correct because just as *all* soldiers may be described as military, all violinists may be described as musical.

WHAT IS A BRIDGE-SENTENCE?

Now let's take a closer look at making up sentences for the key words in an analogy problem. The sentences that we made in the last section formed something like a bridge between the two key words. Just as a bridge joins two shores of a river, each of our sentences joined the key words in a simple sentence that made sense. That's why we call this type of sentence a *Bridge-Sentence*.

Using the Key Words in Reverse Order

Sometimes it's easier to construct a bridge-sentence by reversing the order of the key words. For example, if you are given the key words BLACKBOARD : CHALK, you might make up a bridge-sentence with the key words reversed. It would read like this:

You use chalk on a blackboard.

Here are some examples of two different ways to construct bridge-sentences for key words:

Key Words	*Sentences*
RADIO : MUSIC	*A radio plays music.*
	or
	Music is played on a radio.
TYPEWRITER : KEYS	*A typewriter has keys.*
	or
	Keys are part of a typewriter.
NECKLACE : BEADS	*A necklace is made up of beads.*
	or
	Beads make up a necklace.
HAMMER : CARPENTER	*A hammer is used by a carpenter.*
	or
	A carpenter uses a hammer.
WRESTLER : POWERFUL	*A wrestler is powerful.*
	or
	The word powerful *describes a wrestler.*

Now let's look at the complete analogy problem containing the key words BLACKBOARD : CHALK.

Problem

BLACKBOARD : CHALK : :
a. music : song
b. grass : lawn
c. ink : pen
d. nail : wood
c. paper : pencil

Bridge-Sentence: You use chalk on a blackboard.

Remember, since the order of the words is reversed in the bridge-sentence for the key words, the order of the words in all the choices must also be reversed when you make up bridge-sentences for them.

Sentences	Analyses
a. *You use a song on music.*	No. This is not true.
b. *You use a lawn on grass.*	This doesn't make sense, either.
c. *You use a pen on ink.*	Never.
d. *You use wood on a nail.*	No. You use a nail on wood.
e. *You use a pencil on paper.*	Yes. This makes sense.

Answer: (e) paper : pencil

Here's another analogy problem.

Problem

ENEMY : FEUD : :
a. meal : eat
b. knowledge : study
c. scene : observe
d. thief : respect
e. rival : quarrel

You might try a bridge-sentence like this:

An enemy is a person with whom you feud.

That's okay, but if you find the phrasing a bit awkward, you reverse the key words, as is done in the following sentence.

Bridge-Sentence: *You feud with an enemy.*

Sentences	Analyses
a. *You eat with a meal.*	No. You eat a meal, but you don't eat *with* a meal.
b. *You study with knowledge.*	When you study you are usually seeking knowledge that you do not have. This sentence, therefore, does not seem like a good choice.
c. *You observe with a scene.*	No. You observe a scene.
d. *You respect with a thief.*	This sentence doesn't make sense.
e. *You quarrel with a rival.*	This fits the pattern of the bridge-sentence exactly, so this is the best choice.

Answer: (e) rival : quarrel

Try one more in this section before we move on. Remember, with all the choices in the problem, use the same pattern that you used for the bridge-sentence for the key words. If you do this, the right answer will be the sentence that makes the best sense. The pair of words in the correct choice will just "click" into place.

Problem

TEAM : PLAYER : :
a. novel : author
b. desert : tree
c. stadium : athlete
d. flag : country
e. platoon : soldier

Bridge-Sentence: *A player is a member of a team.*

Sentences	Analyses
a. *An author is a member of a novel.*	Doesn't fit. An author writes a novel.
b. *A tree is a member of a desert.*	No. A tree isn't found in a desert.
c. *An athlete is a member of a stadium.*	An athlete performs in a stadium, but he or she is not a member of it.
d. *A country is a member of a flag.*	Definitely not.
e. *A soldier is a member of a platoon.*	Correct. These words "click" into place. They make perfect sense in the pattern of the bridge-sentence for the key words.

Answer: (e) platoon : soldier

PRACTICE

Writing Bridge-Sentences

On the lines below, write two bridge-sentences for each pair of key words. Write your first sentence in the original order of the key words. In the second sentence, reverse the order of the key words.

1. PAMPHLET : BOOK

   (1) _____

   (2) _____

2. ELEPHANT : JUNGLE

   (1) _____

   (2) _____

3. DIRECTOR : FILM

   (1) _____

   (2) _____

4. FENCE : PROPERTY

   (1) _____

   (2) _____

5. VICTORY : DEFEAT

   (1) _____

   (2) _____

6. EXTINGUISH : FIRE

   (1) _____

   (2) _____

7. FUNERAL : SADNESS

   (1) _____

   (2) _____

8. ROADMAP : MOTORIST

   (1) _____

   (2) _____

9. MOIST : DRENCHED

   (1) _____

   (2) _____

10. YOUNG : INFANTILE

    (1) _____

    (2) _____

11. EDUCATE : TEACH

    (1) _____

    (2) _____

12. BROOK : RIVER

    (1) _____

    (2) _____

13. AMUSING : HILARIOUS

    (1) _____

    (2) _____

14. COWARD : FEAR

    (1) _____

    (2) _____

15. PUZZLE : SOLVE

    (1) _____

    (2) _____

16. MASTER : SLAVE

    (1) _____

    (2) _____

17. GENTLEMAN : POLITE

    (1) _____

    (2) _____

18. HEALTH : ILLNESS

    (1) _____

    (2) _____

19. DOOR : KNOB

    (1) _____

    (2) _____

20. CAUTIOUS : CAREFUL

    (1) _____

    (2) _____

21. FURIOUS : ANNOYED

    (1) _____

    (2) _____

22. POWER : STRENGTH

    (1) _____

    (2) _____

23. STAR : SKY

    (1) _____

    (2) _____

24. OBSERVE : EYE

    (1) _____

    (2) _____

25. JEWELS : SAFE

    (1) _____

    (2) _____

What Do You Do with Words
That Have More Than One Meaning?

Sometimes you can run into trouble in analogy problem solving when you encounter a word that has two or even three meanings. When this happens, you must decide which meaning is called for. Sometimes you need to know whether the word is a noun, verb, or adjective.

Suppose you encounter *address* as a key word. You have to ask yourself: "Does *address* mean *to give a speech* as the President of the United States might do on television? Or, does it mean *the place where someone lives*?" (In the first meaning, *address* is a verb; in the second meaning, *address* is a noun.)

How about the word *exploit*? Does it refer to an *adventure* such as Columbus had when he discovered America? (This meaning would be a noun.) Or, does it mean *to take advantage of someone* by doing something like paying a laborer too little? (This meaning would make *exploit* a verb.)

So, you have to be very careful—and ready to change your bridge-sentence if the first one you try doesn't work with the key words.

Let's look at some examples.

Problem

CHEER : HAPPY : :
a. gloom : sad
b. knowledge : study
c. luck : gamble
d. food : hungry
e. satisfaction : work

At first, you might use *cheer* as a verb and make this bridge-sentence:

You cheer when you're happy.

Then you would have to fit all the choices into this pattern.

You gloom when you're sad.
You knowledge when you study.
You luck when you gamble.
You food when you're hungry.
You satisfaction when you work.

Not one of these makes sense, so you must try another approach. If you look again at the key words, you'll see that *cheer* can also be a noun. After you realize this fact, you make up another bridge-sentence.

You have cheer when you're happy.

Now let's try all the choices in the problem in the revised bridge-sentence.

Sentences	Analyses
a. *You have gloom when you're sad.*	This makes sense. Save it, and look at all the other choices.
b. *You have knowledge when you study.*	Not necessarily. Sometimes you try to learn something, but it is too difficult for you.

10

c. *You have luck when you gamble.*	Not always!
d. *You have food when you're hungry.*	Unfortunately, this is not true for all people.
e. *You have satisfaction when you work.*	Not always.

Answer: (a) gloom : sad

Here's one more analogy problem to look at.

Problem

ACT : PLAY : :
a. soup : wet
b. flower : earth
c. book : page
d. helmet : head
e. stanza : poem

Using *act* as a verb, you might make up the following bridge-sentence.

> *You act in a play.*

Then fit all the choices into this pattern.

> *You soup in a wet.*
> *You flower in the earth.*
> *You book in a page.*
> *You helmet in a head.*
> *You stanza in a poem.*

Since none of these works, you must try something else. If you try *act* as a noun, you come up with the following sentence.

> *An act is part of a play.*

Now try all the choices in the problem in this second pattern.

Sentences	Analyses
a. *A soup is part of wet.*	This makes no sense.
b. *A flower is part of the earth.*	Not exactly. A flower grows in earth.
c. *A book is part of a page.*	No. A page is part of a book.
d. *A helmet is part of a head.*	A helmet is worn on a head, but it is not part of the head.
e. *A stanza is part of a poem.*	Yes. This is true.

Answer: (e) stanza : poem

PRACTICE

Words With More Than One Meaning

Look up the following words in your dictionary and you will find that each has more than one meaning. Enter two different meanings for each word in the spaces provided and write the part of speech (noun, verb, adjective) next to the definition.

1. PRODUCE (1) _____

   (2) _____

2. EXECUTE (1) _____

   (2) _____

3. INITIAL (1) _____

   (2) _____

4. MINUTE (1) _____

   (2) _____

5. REFUSE (1) _____

   (2) _____

6. PERMIT (1) _____

   (2) _____

7. CONVENTION (1) _____

   (2) _____

8. PUPIL (1) _____

   (2) _____

9. NOVEL (1) _____

   (2) _____

10. DISCHARGE (1) _____

    (2) _____

Now that you've gotten the idea, let's try some words with *three* meanings.

11. SPRING (1) _____

    (2) _____

    (3) _____

12. NOTE   (1) _____

                   (2) _____

                   (3) _____

13. BAR   (1) _____

                   (2) _____

                   (3) _____

14. BOLT   (1) _____

                   (2) _____

                   (3) _____

15. FOIL   (1) _____

                   (2) _____

                   (3) _____

16. RULE   (1) _____

                   (2) _____

                   (3) _____

17. BATTER   (1) _____

                   (2) _____

                   (3) _____

18. SCALE   (1) _____

                   (2) _____

                   (3) _____

19. DRILL   (1) _____

                   (2) _____

                   (3) _____

20. PICK   (1) _____

                   (2) _____

                   (3) _____

WHAT ARE TWO-STEP ANALOGIES?

As you might guess, two-step analogies are ones that require you to take two steps to solve them. They are "trickier" than the one-step analogies that we've looked at so far. In a two-step analogy, more than one choice seems at first to be correct. More than one choice fits the pattern of the bridge-sentence used for the key words.

Example

Problem

CLASS : TEACHER : :
a. court : lawyer
b. bus : driver
c. store : salesperson
d. principal : school
e. team : coach

Step 1: Bridge Sentence: *A teacher takes charge of a class.*

Sentences	Analyses
a. *A lawyer takes charge of a court.*	Incorrect. A judge takes charge of a court.
b. *A driver takes charge of a bus.*	Could be correct. Make your final decision later.
c. *A salesperson takes charge of a store.*	No. The manager takes charge.
d. *A school takes charge of a principal.*	No. It's just the opposite. A principal takes charge of a school.
e. *A coach takes charge of a team.*	This seems correct too.

Choices *b* and *e* both seem correct, so you have to go on to Step 2 to find the best answer of the two possibilities.

Step 2: Now you must look more closely at the two possibilities and compare them to the key words more carefully.

Choice b: At first it may seem that a bus driver takes charge of a bus in the same way that a teacher takes charge of a class. But there is some difference. A teacher takes charge of a class in a *general* sense. However, a bus driver does not take charge of the bus in a *general* sense. For example, he or she does not plan the route. He does drive the bus, but, in general, the bus driver carries out many orders and rules made by other people.

Choice 3: A coach is more like a teacher than a bus driver is. A coach takes charge of a team in a general way by directing and instructing. Indeed, a coach is a kind of teacher.

Answer: (e) team : coach

Now let's try another two-step analogy.

Problem

WRESTLER : ARENA : :
a. bird : nest
b. traveler : plane
c. runner : race
d. businessperson : office
e. football player : stadium

Step 1: Bridge-Sentence: *A wrestler is in an arena.*

Sentences	Analyses
a. *A bird is in a nest.*	Sounds alright.
b. *A traveler is in a plane.*	Sometimes.
c. *A runner is in a race.*	Maybe.
d. *A businessperson is in an office.*	Sometimes.
e. *A football player is in a stadium.*	During the game.

Step 2: Step 1 showed you that all five choices are possibilities. This means that in Step 2 you must take a closer look at all the choices and compare them more carefully to the key words.

One thing to notice right away is that the key words and all possible choices, except *a*, are about people. Since *a* is different, eliminate it as a choice.

Then you should see that the key words are not only about people, they are about athletes. Of the remaining possible choices (*b*, *c*, *d*, and *e*), both *c* and *e* are about athletes, so keep them as possibilities and reject *b* and *d*.

Now you must decide which is closer to the key words, *b* or *d*. Notice that the key words tell you where a wrestler performs (in an arena). Choice *e* tells you where a football player performs, but Choice *c* does not tell you where a runner performs. (A *race* is not a place like a *stadium* is or like an *arena* is.)

Answer: (e) football player : stadium

Now let's look at three more two-step analogy problems.

1. Problem

BABY : CHILD : :
a. girl : woman
b. cub : bear
c. uncle : cousin
d. country : continent
e. film : movie

Step 1: Bridge-Sentence: *A baby becomes a child.*

Sentences	Analyses
a. *A girl becomes a woman.*	Sounds right.
b. *A cub becomes a bear.*	Also sounds right.
c. *An uncle becomes a cousin.*	No.
d. *A country becomes a continent.*	No. This doesn't happen.
e. *A film becomes a movie.*	No. A film *is* a movie.

Both *a* and *b* seem correct, so you must go on to Step 2.

Step 2: Look at the key words and you will see that they refer to the growth of a human being. Choice *a* refers to the growth of a human being, but Choice *b* refers to the growth of an animal.

Answer: (a) girl : woman

---

2. Problem

COLLAR : NECK : :
a. overcoat : body
b. wrist : watch
c. belt : waist
d. zipper : sweater
e. fence : property

Step 1: Bridge-Sentence: *A collar goes around a neck.*

Sentences	Analyses
a. *An overcoat goes around a body.*	Not exactly. An overcoat covers a body, but it does not encircle it.
b. *A wrist goes around a watch.*	No. Just the reverse. A watch goes around a wrist.
c. *A belt goes around a waist.*	Sounds good.
d. *A zipper goes around a sweater.*	Not usually.
e. *A fence goes around property.*	This is often true.

Both *c* and *e* seem to fit the bridge-sentence, so look again at the key words.

Step 2: *Collar* refers to *clothes,* and so does *belt. Fence* does not.

Answer: (c) belt : waist

Answers and Explanations for Warm-Up 1

Answers

1. b 2. e 3. d 4. e 5. a 6. b 7. a 8. e 9. c 10. d

Explanations

1. Answer (b) ribbon : cloth

   Problem
   CHAIN : METAL : :
   a. newspaper : events
   b. ribbon : cloth
   c. house : stone
   d. tie : stripes
   e. cigarette: tobacco

   Bridge-Sentence for Key Words
   A chain is made completely of metal.
   (Also, a chain has a long, thin shape.)

   Bridge-Sentence for Answer
   A ribbon is made completely of cloth.
   (A ribbon also has a long, thin shape.)

   Comments about the Other Choices
   a. A newspaper is not made up of events printed on a page.
   c. A house may be made of stone, but it would not have a long, thin shape.
   d. A tie may have stripes on it, but it is not *made* of stripes.
   e. A cigarette does contain tobacco, but it is not made completely of tobacco.

2. Answer (e) butter : bread

   Problem
   CHEESE : CRACKERS : :
   a. spoon : fork
   b. candy : wrapper
   c. belt : pants
   d. cookie : snack
   e. butter : bread

   Bridge-Sentence for Key Words
   Cheese is spread on crackers.
   (and eaten)

   Bridge-Sentence for Answer
   Butter is spread on bread.
   (and eaten)

   Comments about the Other Choices
   a. A spoon and fork are not foods.
   b. Candy is wrapped in a wrapper.
   c. A belt and pants are not foods.
   d. A cookie *is* a snack.

3. Answer (d) fish : scales

   Problem
   CHICKEN : FEATHERS : :
   a. elephant : trunk
   b. tiger : claws
   c. fur : bear
   d. fish : scales
   e. parakeet : cage

   Bridge-Sentence for Key Words
   A chicken is covered with feathers.

   Bridge-Sentence for Answer
   A fish is covered with scales.

   Comments about the Other Choices
   a. An elephant is not covered with a trunk.
   b. A tiger is not covered with claws.
   c. A bear is covered with fur, but this reverses the order of the words.
   e. A parakeet lives in a cage.

4. Answer (e) car : garage

Problem
HORSE : STABLE : :
a. boat : ocean
b. airplane : clouds
c. diamond : ring
d. walrus : ice
e. car : garage

Bridge-Sentence for Key Words
A horse is kept in a stable.
(something kept in a specific place)

Bridge-Sentence for Answer
A car is kept in a garage.
(something kept in a specific place)

Comments about the Other Choices
a. A boat sails on the ocean.
b. An airplane flies through the clouds.
c. A diamond is sometimes a part of a ring.
d. A walrus lives and travels on ice.
None of the above (a, b, c, or d) is something kept in a specific place.

5. Answer (a) scatter : apart

Problem
GATHER : TOGETHER : :
a. scatter : apart
b. practice : display
c. tell : explain
d. organize : finish
e. discover : travel

Bridge-Sentence for Key Words
When you gather, things move to-gether.

Bridge-Sentence for Answer
When you scatter, things move apart.

Comments about the Other Choices
None of the other choices fits the pattern of the bridge-sentence.

6. Answer (b) mountain : hill

Problem
GIANT : DWARF : :
a. kind : cruel
b. mountain : hill
c. elf : monster
d. child : father
e. stream : river

Bridge-Sentence for Key Words
A giant is much larger than a dwarf.
(The emphasis here is on size.)

Bridge-Sentence for Answer
A mountain is much larger than a hill.
(The emphasis here is on size.)

Comments about the Other Choices
a. *Kind* and *cruel* do not relate to physical size.
c. The main difference between an elf and a monster is not size.
d. *Child* and *father* relate to size, but the word order is wrong for the pattern of the bridge-sentence.
e. A stream is smaller than a river, not larger.

7. Answer (a) shelf : book

Problem
HOOK : COAT : :
a. shelf : book
b. laundry : shirt
c. mouth : gum
d. diamond : baseball
e. ring : round

Bridge-Sentence for Key Words
The coat is on the hook.
(The hook is *holding* the coat.)

Bridge-Sentence for Answer
The book is on the shelf.
(The shelf is *holding* the book.)

Comments about the Other Choices

Remember, since the order of the key words has been reversed in the bridge-sentence, the order of the words in all the choices must also be reversed.

b. The shirt is not *on* the laundry.
c. Gum would be *in* the mouth, not *on* the mouth.
d. A baseball might be on the diamond, but the diamond would not be *holding* the baseball.
e. The words *ring* and *round* do not fit the pattern of the bridge-sentence.

8. Answer (e) scribble : write

Problem
CRAWL : WALK : :
a. grow : born
b. swim : float
c. swallow : chew
d. listen : agree
e. scribble : write

Bridge-Sentence for Key Words
First you crawl, and then you walk.
(a natural sequence of events)

Bridge-Sentence for Answer
First you scribble, and then you write.
(a natural sequence of events)

Comments about the Other Choices
a. The words are in the wrong order to fit the bridge-sentence pattern.
b. This is not necessarily a natural sequence of events.
c. These actions are not a natural sequence.
d. You don't necessarily agree after you listen.

9. Answer (c) puppy : dog

Problem
CALF : COW : :
a. cat : kitten
b. woman : girl
c. puppy : dog
d. shower : storm
e. path : road

Bridge-Sentence for Key Words
A calf grows into a cow.
(a living being)

Bridge-Sentence for Answer
A puppy grows into a dog.
(a living being)

Comments about the Other Choices
a. The words in this choice are in the wrong order.
b. The words in this choice are in the wrong order too.
d. These words do not refer to a living being.
e. *Path* and *road* do not deal with growing in a physical sense.

10. Answer (d) whisper : soft

Problem
SHOUT : LOUD : :
a. laugh : happy
b. sad : cry
c. smile : friendly
d. whisper : soft
e. exercise : energetic

Bridge-Sentence for Key Words
A shout is loud.
(relates to volume or level of sound)

Bridge-Sentence for Answer
A whisper is soft.
(relates to volume or level of sound)

Comments about the Other Choices
a. A laugh is happy, but *happy* does not deal with volume of sound.
b. When *sad* is used to describe *cry*, the emphasis is not on sound.
c. *Smile* and *friendly* do not deal with sound.
e. Exercise may be energetic, but it is not related to sound.

WARM-UP 2

Directions: Select the pair of words that most nearly expresses the relationship of the pair of key words in capital letters. Circle the letter preceding the pair you choose. Write a bridge-sentence on the lines provided before selecting your answer.

1. BOY : HANDSOME : :
   a. girl : pretty
   b. grandmother : kind
   c. cat : black
   d. scenery : nature
   e. woman : old

   Bridge-Sentence _____

   _____

2. GUEST : HOTEL : :
   a. soldier : army
   b. fish : person
   c. patient : hospital
   d. pupil : school
   e. baby : crib

   _____

   _____

3. MARKET : FOOD : :
   a. clinic : disease
   b. post office : mail
   c. pharmacy : drugs
   d. museum : paintings
   e. customer : shop

   _____

   _____

4. LETTERS : WORDS : :
   a. pages : paragraphs
   b. sentences : paragraphs
   c. colors : writing
   d. tiles : floors
   e. cars : highways

   _____

   _____

5. QUESTION : ANSWER : :
   a. travel : rest
   b. hide : seek
   c. forget : recall
   d. add : subtract
   e. ask : reply

   _____

   _____

6. CIRCLE : ROUND : :
   a. dot : black
   b. star : bright
   c. line : straight
   d. box : big
   e. dictionary : heavy

   _____

   _____

7. ADD : SUBTRACT : :
   a. school : vacation
   b. count : spell
   c. build : destroy
   d. work : play
   e. multiply : divide

   _____

   _____

8. ARROW : BOW : :
   a. bullet : rifle
   b. ball : paddle
   c. curtain : window
   d. pizza : cheese
   e. buckle : belt

   _____

   _____

9. ARTIST : PAINT : :
   a. secretary : dictate
   b. child : scribble
   c. waiter : serve
   d. author : write
   e. diner : eat

   _____

   _____

10. BRAVE : COURAGE : :
    a. old : years
    b. bright : glow
    c. afraid : fear
    d. intelligent : money
    e. healthy : muscle

    _____

    _____

Answers and Explanations for Warm-Up 2

Answers

1. a 2. c 3. c 4. b 5. e 6. c 7. e 8. a. 9. d 10. c

Explanations

1. Answer (a) girl : pretty

   Problem
   BOY : HANDSOME : :
   a. girl : pretty
   b. grandmother : kind
   c. cat : black
   d. scenery : nature
   e. woman : old

   Bridge-Sentence for Key Words
   A boy may be a handsome person.
   (relates to physical appearance)

   Bridge-Sentence for Answer
   A girl may be a pretty person.
   (relates to physical appearance)

   Comments about the Other Choices
   b. A grandmother may be a kind person, but the emphasis here is on personality, not physical appearance.
   c. A cat may be black, but it's an animal, not a person.
   d. Scenery relates to nature, not to a person.
   e. A woman may be old, but the emphasis here is on age rather than physical appearance.

2. Answer (c) patient : hospital

   Problem
   GUEST : HOTEL : :
   a. soldier : army
   b. fish : person
   c. patient : hospital
   d. pupil : school
   e. baby : crib

   Bridge-Sentence for Key Words
   A guest lives temporarily in a hotel.
   (The emphasis is on residing in a building.)

   Bridge-Sentence for Answer
   A patient lives temporarily in a hospital.
   (The emphasis is on residing in a building.)

   Comments about the Other Choices
   a. An army is not a building.
   b. A fish does not live in a person.
   d. A pupil attends a school, but he or she does not live there in any sense.
   e. A baby may stay in a crib for a while, but in no way does a baby live in a crib.

3. Answer (c) pharmacy : drugs

   Problem
   MARKET : FOOD : :
   a. clinic : disease
   b. post office : mail
   c. pharmacy : drugs
   d. museum : paintings
   e. customer : shop

   Bridge-Sentence for Key Words
   A market sells food.
   (store and product)

   Bridge-Sentence for Answer
   A pharmacy sells drugs.
   (store and product)

Comments about the Other Choices
a. A clinic does not sell disease.
b. A post office does not sell mail.
d. A museum exhibits paintings; it does not sell them.
e. A customer buys something in a shop; the customer does not sell the shop.

4. Answer (b) sentences : paragraphs

Problem
LETTERS : WORDS : :
a. pages : paragraphs
b. sentences : paragraphs
c. colors : writing
d. tiles : floors
e. cars : highways

Bridge-Sentence for Key Words
Letters make up words.
(relates to writing)

Bridge-Sentence for Answer
Sentences make up paragraphs.
(relates to writing)

Comments about the Other Choices
a. Both of these words relate to writing, but pages do not make up paragraphs.
c. Colors are not related to writing.
d. Tiles and floors are not related to writing.
e. Cars do not make up highways.

5. Answer (e) ask : reply

Problem
QUESTION : ANSWER : :
a. travel : rest
b. hide : seek
c. forget : recall
d. add : subtract
e. ask : reply

Bridge-Sentence for Key Words
If you question, you may get an answer.
(relates to speech)

Bridge-Sentence for Answer
If you ask, you may get a reply.
(relates to speech)

Comments about the Other Choices
a. Travel and rest are not related to speech.
b. These words do not fit the pattern of the bridge-sentence.
c. These words do not fit the pattern of the bridge-sentence.
d. Add and subtract are not related to speech.

6. Answer (c) line : straight

Problem
CIRCLE : ROUND : :
a. dot : black
b. star : bright
c. line : straight
d. box : big
e. dictionary : heavy

Bridge-Sentence for Key Words
A circle is round.
(relates to shape)

Bridge-Sentence for Answer
A line is straight.
(relates to shape)

Comments about the Other Choices
a. A dot may be black, but the emphasis is not on shape here.
b. Although a star may be bright, brightness does not relate to shape.
d. A box may be big or small; this choice relates to size, not shape.
e. The words *dictionary* and *heavy* do not relate to shape.

7. Answer (e) multiply : divide

Problem
ADD : SUBTRACT : :
a. school : vacation
b. count : spell
c. build : destroy
d. work : play
e. multiply : divide

Bridge-Sentence for Key Words
Add is the opposite of subtract.
(a mathematical relationship)

Bridge-Sentence for Answer
Multiply is the opposite of divide.
(a mathematical relationship)

Comments about the Other Choices
Choices *a*, *c*, and *d* all can be viewed as opposites, but none of these relates to a mathematical relationship.
b. *Count* and *spell* are not opposites.

8. Answer (a) bullet : rifle

Problem
ARROW : BOW : :
a. bullet : rifle
b. ball : paddle
c. curtain : window
d. pizza : cheese
e. buckle : belt

Bridge-Sentence for Key Words
A bow shoots an arrow.
(These words can be related to weapons.)

Bridge-Sentence for Answer
A rifle shoots a bullet.
(These words can be related to weapons.)

Comments about the Other Choices
Note that the order of words has been reversed in the bridge-sentence for the key words. This means that the order of words must be reversed in all the other choices as well.

None of the choices except *a* fits the bridge sentence. No other choice can use the word *shoot* (as you would with a weapon) in it.

9. Answer (d) author : write

Problem
ARTIST : PAINT : :
a. secretary : dictate
b. child : scribble
c. waiter : serve
d. author : write
e. diner : eat

Bridge-Sentence for Key Words
An artist will paint.
(This is a creative, cultural activity.)

Bridge-Sentence for Answer
An author will write.
(This too is a creative, cultural activity.)

Comments about the Other Choices
a. A secretary usually will not dictate; someone dictates to the secretary.
b. A child may scribble. Some people might see this as creative, but it would not be considered cultural.
c. A waiter may serve, but again this activity would not be considered creative and cultural.
e. A diner may eat, but, like some of the other choices, this activity would not be considered creative and cultural.

10. Answer (c) afraid : fear

Problem
BRAVE : COURAGE : :
a. old : years
b. bright : glow
c. afraid : fear
d. intelligent : money
e. healthy : muscle

Bridge-Sentence for Key Words
If you're brave, you have courage.
(a personal quality)

Bridge-Sentence for Answer
If you're afraid, you have fear.
(a personal quality)

Comments about the Other Choices
a. *Old* and *years* do not relate to personal qualities.
b. A person would not glow because of being bright.
d. *Intelligence* and *money* do not relate to personal qualities.
e. The words in this choice refer to physical, not personal, qualities.

WARM-UP 3

Directions: Select the pair of words that most nearly expresses the relationship of the pair of key words in capital letters. Circle the letter preceding the pair you choose. Write a bridge-sentence on the lines provided before selecting your answer.

1. ANKLE : LEG : :
   a. hat : head
   b. brain : heart
   c. battery : radio
   d. face : nose
   e. elbow : arm

   Bridge-Sentence _____

   _____

2. CEREAL : BOX : :
   a. trunk : elephant
   b. lawn : house
   c. plumbing : sink
   d. money : pocket
   e. ice cream : flavor

   _____

   _____

3. BROOM : FLOOR : :
   a. polish : floor
   b. dish : cloth
   c. rake : leaves
   d. lawnmower : grass
   e. toothbrush : teeth

   _____

   _____

4. BREAKFAST : MORNING : :
   a. oatmeal : milk
   b. supper : evening
   c. turkey : Thanksgiving
   d. lunch : school
   e. snack : cafeteria

   _____

   _____

5. SHEET : CLOTH : :
   a. board : wood
   b. ruler : inches
   c. beach : shells
   d. sky : clouds
   e. glass : window

   _____

   _____

6. BRAIN : THINK : :
   a. briefcase : carry
   b. heart : attack
   c. airplane : fly
   d. crayon : draw
   e. stomach : digest

   _____

   _____

7. BOAT : SAIL : :
   a. bicycle : rider
   b. shoemaker : hammer
   c. airplane : wing
   d. ship : captain
   e. train : tracks

   _____

   _____

8. LIE : BED : :
   a. study : school
   b. play : game
   c. ride : bus
   d. table : eat
   e. sit : chair

   _____

   _____

9. CUP : BOWL : :
   a. spoon : fork
   b. tie : shirt
   c. ring : tire
   d. principal : school
   e. branch : tree

   _____

   _____

10. DISTANT : CLOSE : :
    a. angry : friendly
    b. hot : warm
    c. far : near
    d. silly : serious
    e. enemy : friend

    _____

    _____

Answers and Explanations for Warm-Up 3

Answers

1. e 2. d 3. e 4. b 5. a 6. e 7. c 8. e 9. c 10. c

Explanations

1. Answer (e) elbow : arm

   Problem
   ANKLE : LEG : :
   a. hat : head
   b. brain : heart
   c. battery : radio
   d. face : nose
   e. elbow : arm

   Bridge-Sentence for Key Words
   An ankle is part of a leg.
   (relates to the body)

   Bridge-Sentence for Answer
   An elbow is part of an arm.
   (relates to the body)

   Comments about the Other Choices
   a. A hat may be on a head, but it is not a part of the head.
   b. *Brain* and *heart* both relate to the body, but the brain is not part of the heart.
   c. A battery may be a part of a radio, but these terms do not relate to the body.
   d. A face is not part of a nose; a nose is part of a face.

2. Answer (d) money : pocket

   Problem
   CEREAL : BOX : :
   a. trunk : elephant
   b. lawn : house
   c. plumbing : sink
   d. money : pocket
   e. ice cream : flavor

   Bridge-Sentence for Key Words
   A box can contain cereal.
   (The idea here is related to keeping something in a particular place for a period of time.)

   Bridge-Sentence for Answer
   A pocket can contain money.
   (Here, too, the idea is to keep something in a particular place for a period of time.)

   Comments about the Other Choices
   Note that the key words have been reversed in the bridge-sentence.
   a. The words in this choice do not fit the pattern of the bridge-sentence.
   b. A house may have a lawn, but it does not contain it.
   c. A sink may contain plumbing but not in the sense of keeping it there for a limited period of time.
   e. A flavor does not contain ice cream.

3. Answer (e) toothbrush : teeth

   Problem
   BROOM : FLOOR : :
   a. polish : floor
   b. dish : cloth
   c. rake : leaves
   d. lawnmower : grass
   e. toothbrush : teeth

   Bridge-Sentence for Key Words
   A broom cleans a floor.
   (an instrument with bristles)

   Bridge-Sentence for Answer
   A toothbrush cleans teeth.
   (an instrument with bristles)

Comments about the Other Choices
a. Polish doesn't actually clean a floor; it makes it shine.
b. A dish does not clean a cloth.
c. A rake may be used to clean leaves from a yard, but the rake does not clean the leaves.
d. A lawnmower doesn't clean grass; it cuts it.

4. Answer (b) supper : evening

Problem
BREAKFAST : MORNING : :
a. oatmeal : milk
b. supper : evening
c. turkey : Thanksgiving
d. lunch : school
e. snack : cafeteria

Bridge-Sentence for Key Words
You eat breakfast in the morning.
(a meal eaten at a particular time)

Bridge-Sentence for Answer
You eat supper in the evening.
(a meal eaten at a particular time)

Comments about the Other Choices
a. These words do not describe a meal eaten at a particular time.
c. Turkey is not a meal, although Thanksgiving is a particular time.
d. Lunch is a meal, but school is not a particular time.
e. You eat a snack in the cafeteria, but a cafeteria is a place, not a time.

5. Answer (a) board : wood

Problem
SHEET : CLOTH : :
a. board : wood
b. ruler : inches
c. beach : shells
d. sky : clouds
e. glass : window

Bridge-Sentence for Key Words
A sheet is made of cloth.
(Cloth is a material.)

Bridge-Sentence for Answer
A board is made of wood.
(Wood is a material.)

Comments about the Other Choices
b. Inches are not a material that makes up a ruler.
c. While a beach may have shells on it, it is not made up of shells. It is made up of sand.
d. Clouds are not a material that makes up the sky.
e. The words in this choice do not work unless they are reversed.

6. Answer (e) stomach : digest

Problem
BRAIN : THINK : :
a. briefcase : carry
b. heart : attack
c. airplane : fly
d. crayon : draw
e. stomach : digest

Bridge-Sentence for Key Words
You think with your brain.
(a part of your body)

Bridge-Sentence for Answer
You digest with your stomach.
(a part of your body)

Comments about the Other Choices
Note that the order of the key words has been reversed in the bridge-sentence for them.
a. You may carry with your briefcase, but a briefcase is not a part of your body.
b. These words do not fit the bridge-sentence.
c. These words do not describe parts of the body.
d. You may draw with your crayon, but these words do not relate to a part of the body.

7. Answer (c) airplane : wing

Problem
BOAT : SAIL : :
a. bicycle : rider
b. shoemaker : hammer
c. airplane : wing
d. ship : captain
e. train : tracks

Bridge-Sentence for Key Words
A sail is part of a boat.
(Both words are objects.)

Bridge-Sentence for Answer
A wing is part of an airplane.
(Both words are objects.)

Comments about the Other Choices
Note that the order of the key words has been reversed in the bridge-sentence.
a. A rider is not an object that is part of a bicycle.
b. These words do not fit the bridge-sentence at all.
d. A captain is not an object that is part of a ship.
e. *Tracks* and *train* are both objects, but tracks are not part of a train.

8. Answer (e) sit : chair

Problem
LIE : BED : :
a. study : school
b. play : game
c. ride : bus
d. table : eat
e. sit : chair

Bridge-Sentence for Key Words
You lie in a bed.
(refers to resting on a piece of furniture)

Bridge-Sentence for Answer
You sit in a chair.
(refers to resting on a piece of furniture)

Comments about the Other Choices
a. You study in a school, but these words do not relate to resting.
b. You play in a game, but these words do not refer to furniture.
c. Riding in a bus is not necessarily resting. Plus, a bus is not a piece of furniture.
d. These words do not fit the bridge-sentence.

9. Answer (c) ring : tire

Problem
CUP : BOWL : :
a. spoon : fork
b. tie : shirt
c. ring : tire
d. principal : school
e. branch : tree

Bridge-Sentence for Key Words
A cup and a bowl have similar shapes.

Bridge-Sentence for Answer
A ring and a tire have similar shapes.

Comments about the Other Choices
No choice except *c* contains words that have similar shapes.

10. Answer (c) far : near

Problem
DISTANT : CLOSE : :
a. angry : friendly
b. hot : warm
c. far : near
d. silly : serious
e. enemy : friend

Bridge-Sentence for Key Words
Distant is the opposite of close.
(refers to location)

Bridge-Sentence for Answer
Far is the opposite of near.
(refers to location)

Comments about the Other Choices
All of the choices in this analogy problem can be viewed as opposites, but only
Choice c refers to location.

UNIT A

Directions: Circle the pair of words that most nearly expresses the relationship of the pair of key words in capital letters.

1. CONGREGATION : CHURCH : :
   a. army : battlefield
   b. audience : theatre
   c. crowd : streets
   d. pitcher : team
   e. chorus : school

2. LAWYER : PROFESSIONAL : :
   a. dictionary : book
   b. burglar : criminal
   c. consumer : salesperson
   d. cook : waiter
   e. sea : ocean

3. INFANT : CHILD : :
   a. pupil : scholar
   b. teacher : principal
   c. adolescent : adult
   d. brother : sister
   e. daughter : mother

4. REVOLT : MUTINY : :
   a. riot : bloodshed
   b. battle : victory
   c. war : disaster
   d. shower : cloudburst
   e. uprising : rebellion

5. PAPER : GLUE : :
   a. scrapbook : souvenirs
   b. link : chain
   c. needle : thread
   d. chain : steel
   e. brick : cement

6. CAR : MOTOR : :
   a. umbrella : handle
   b. engine : iron
   c. truck : tire
   d. candle : holder
   e. flashlight : battery

7. KITCHEN : LINOLEUM : :
   a. building : cement
   b. lawn : grass
   c. highway : cars
   d. parlor : carpet
   e. tent : earth

8. BEACON : SAILOR : :
   a. nutrition : athlete
   b. lamp : reader
   c. horse : cowboy
   d. pipe : smoker
   e. advertisement : public

9. TOOL : MECHANIC : :
   a. piano : musician
   b. luck : gambler
   c. program : usher
   d. utensil : cook
   e. chart : sailor

10. PAINTER : EASEL : :
    a. child : crayon
    b. cook : recipe
    c. waiter : tray
    d. dietician : vitamin
    e. commander : garrison

11. SOIL : FERTILE : :
    a. author : prolific
    b. congressman : busy
    c. clerk : efficient
    d. government : powerful
    e. runner : exhausted

12. OBEY : REGULATION : :
    a. recall : incident
    b. disobey : law
    c. add : amendment
    d. follow : order
    e. obtain : permission

13. GLOSSARY : WORDS : :
    a. album : pictures
    b. index : pages
    c. list : people
    d. play : actors
    e. cookbook : recipes

14. NEAT : UNTIDY : :
    a. organized : efficient
    b. correct : accurate
    c. elderly : ancient
    d. orderly : haphazard
    e. sanitary : medical

15. COUNTERFEIT : IMITATION : :
    a. photography : drawing
    b. replica : reproduction
    c. copy : letter
    d. shadow : person
    e. twin : brother

16. BURGLAR : STEAL : :
    a. guard : watch
    b. thief : flee
    c. shoplifter : pilfer
    d. policeofficer : arrest
    e. convict : escape

17. SCROLL : WRITE : :
    a. knife : carve
    b. pen : draw
    c. studio : paint
    d. tombstone : engrave
    e. cheek : scratch

18. MARATHON : ODYSSEY : :
    a. race : journey
    b. contest : battle
    c. run : march
    d. hike : stroll
    e. sports : studies

19. HERMIT : SOLITARY : :
    a. outcast : alone
    b. defendant : guilty
    c. prisoner : innocent
    d. exile : regretful
    e. designer : creative

20. CLOTH : REMNANT : :
    a. paper : scrap
    b. thread : spool
    c. tin : can
    d. door : lock
    e. wood : pile

UNIT B

Directions: Circle the pair of words that most nearly expresses the relationship of the pair of key words in capital letters.

1. QUESTION : ANSWER : :
   a. inquire : reply
   b. respond : declare
   c. suggest : hint
   d. ask : beg
   e. request : invite

2. CADDY : JOCKEY : :
   a. horse : club
   b. boy : man
   c. golf : horse racing
   d. tall : short
   e. course : stadium

3. WORKER : UNION : :
   a. president : nation
   b. pupil : classroom
   c. stamp : collection
   d. painting : museum
   e. member : club

4. COUNTRY : BORDER : :
   a. picture : frame
   b. story : beginning
   c. building : wall
   d. government : constitution
   e. trousers : belt

5. DISAGREE : ARGUE : :
   a. consent : desire
   b. differ : debate
   c. challenge : fight
   d. witness : lie
   e. enjoy : agree

6. ANIMAL : HIDE : :
   a. tree : trunk
   b. lizard : tail
   c. person : skin
   d. body : skeleton
   e. flower : petal

7. CONTOUR : BODY : :
   a. landscape : mountain
   b. tire : wheel
   c. glow : star
   d. suburb : city
   e. outline : drawing

8. CRIMINAL : ALIAS : :
   a. product : trademark
   b. soldier : weapon
   c. author : pen name
   d. word : synonym
   e. celebrity : reputation

9. GUESS : PROOF : :
   a. erroneous : correct
   b. conjecture : certainty
   c. question : answer
   d. possibility : probability
   e. honesty : truth

10. COLOR : FADE : :
    a. pillow : comfort
    b. wine : age
    c. liquid : evaporate
    d. elastic : expand
    e. flower : wither

11. UNCOUTH : BEHAVIOR : :
    a. rude : manner
    b. tolerant : attitude
    c. discourteous : remark
    d. offensive : odor
    e. cheerful : personality

12. APATHY : CARE : :
    a. sympathy : feeling
    b. certainty : confidence
    c. unity : strength
    d. poverty : money
    e. loyalty : devotion

13. SNIP : STRING : :
    a. break : chain
    b. sever : rope
    c. tie : ribbon
    d. tear : page
    e. slice : loaf

14. CAUTION : PITFALL : :
    a. exercise : illness
    b. determination : success
    c. alertness : sleep
    d. learning : ignorance
    e. care : blunder

15. FORETELL : FUTURE : :
    a. await : tomorrow
    b. reminisce : past
    c. plan : ahead
    d. run : advance
    e. write : history

16. FICKLE : PERSONALITY : :
    a. declining : demand
    b. melting : ice
    c. changeable : weather
    d. constant : pleasure
    e. rising : prices

17. TERMINATION : END : :
    a. invigorate : health
    b. enjoy : pleasure
    c. creation : beginning
    d. initiate : open
    e. organize : growth

18. WANDERER : RAMBLE : :
    a. smoker : inhale
    b. voyager : travel
    c. jogger : train
    d. sprinter : dash
    e. explorer : sail

19. CONTRADICT : CONCUR : :
    a. assert : admit
    b. rebut : agree
    c. congratulate : praise
    d. support : uphold
    e. accumulate : distribute

20. FOOL : GULLIBLE : :
    a. glutton : sociable
    b. diplomat : elderly
    c. agent : legal
    d. reporter : magazine
    e. brother : fraternal

UNIT C

Directions: Circle the pair of words that most nearly expresses the relationship of the pair of key words in capital letters.

1. MILK : LIQUID : :
   a. iron : metal
   b. dirt : brown
   c. wood : flat
   d. ocean : deep
   e. knife : sharp

2. MINORITY : SMALL : :
   a. charity : kind
   b. totality : gigantic
   c. catastrophe : tragic
   d. majority : large
   e. authority : strict

3. BUILDER : CONSTRUCT : :
   a. worker : haul
   b. artist : organize
   c. chef : taste
   d. motorist : travel
   e. architect : plan

4. KING : REIGN : :
   a. student : school
   b. president : term
   c. stenographer : office
   d. queen : palace
   e. calendar : year

5. WORSHIP : SHRINE : :
   a. dwell : cottage
   b. climb : mountain
   c. pray : church
   d. learn : university
   e. study : library

6. AGREE : SUGGESTION : :
   a. reject : amendments
   b. accept : offer
   c. destroy : opponent
   d. add : supply
   e. include : item

7. SQUAD : ARMY : :
   a. grove : forest
   b. male : female
   c. café : restaurant
   d. submarine : navy
   e. group : horde

8. CURSE : HATE : :
   a. insult : dislike
   b. frown : resent
   c. refer : object
   d. dismiss : separate
   e. praise : worship

9. PERUSE : CONTRACT : :
   a. evaluate : performance
   b. scribble : reply
   c. consider : temptation
   d. glance : note
   e. observe : regulation

10. GUST : WIND : :
    a. spark : flicker
    b. snowflake : blizzard
    c. breeze : hurricane
    d. typhoon : cyclone
    e. island : continent

11. BLUNDER : WRONG : :
    a. mistake : serious
    b. lie : untruthful
    c. error : incorrect
    d. idea : disastrous
    e. disaster : unusual

12. SURMOUNT : OBSTACLE : :
    a. light : beacon
    b. mourn : misfortune
    c. overcome : handicap
    d. verify : fact
    e. assault : barrier

13. IRATE : SPEECH : :
    a. musical : tone
    b. heated : argument
    c. soft : voice
    d. brief : comment
    e. different : opinion

14. SMUGGLER : ILLICIT : :
    a. sheriff : legal
    b. garrison : heroic
    c. crime : unlawful
    d. thief : cautious
    e. detective : observant

15. STADIUM : IMMENSE : :
    a. ring : sound
    b. classroom : educational
    c. huge : building
    d. city : ancient
    e. closet : small

16. DECADE : CENTURY : :
    a. penny : nickel
    b. hour : day
    c. dime : dollar
    d. month : year
    e. ounce : pound

17. HEALTHY : MORBID : :
    a. pleasant : morbid
    b. forceful : vehement
    c. contaminated : filthy
    d. infantile : mature
    e. wholesome : sickly

18. DONOR : GIVE : :
    a. statesman : negotiate
    b. sportswoman : compete
    c. newspaper : advertising
    d. host : entertain
    e. beneficiary : receive

19. ENCORE : AFTER : :
    a. intermission : lengthy
    b. introduction : friendly
    c. poster : creative
    d. product : reliable
    e. prelude : before

20. EXPERT : CONNOISSEUR : :
    a. attorney : lawyer
    b. pupil : juvenile
    c. class : teacher
    d. professional : amateur
    e. supervisor : colleague

UNIT D

Directions: Circle the pair of words that most nearly expresses the relationship of the pair of key words in capital letters.

1. GRASS : GROUND : :
   a. eye : nose
   b. nail : finger
   c. profile : face
   d. toe : leg
   e. hair : head

2. FEUD : FAMILIES : :
   a. game : competitors
   b. war : nations
   c. divorce : wives
   d. match : players
   e. competition : contestants

3. PARTY : POLITICS : :
   a. recreation : study
   b. celebration : mourning
   c. cult : religion
   d. Saturday : Sunday
   e. person : individual

4. INAUGURATE : PRESIDENT : :
   a. nominate : candidate
   b. refuse : offer
   c. crown : king
   d. decide : issue
   e. pick : winner

5. BOOKS : LIBRARY : :
   a. depositors : bank
   b. shoppers : mall
   c. pages : book
   d. pictures : gallery
   e. stamps : letter

6. EVACUATE : LEAVE : :
   a. discontinue : alter
   b. assault : attack
   c. celebrate : cheer
   d. originate : organize
   e. retreat : withdraw

7. ATHLETE : ROBUST : :
   a. boxer : strong
   b. surfer : wet
   c. treasurer : reliable
   d. acrobat : handsome
   e. grocer : friendly

8. SEDATE : DIGNIFIED : :
   a. official : efficient
   b. courteous : considerate
   c. insistent : demanding
   d. immature : infantile
   e. ignorant : rude

9. GIFT : RECEIVE : :
   a. present : purchase
   b. interest : develop
   c. permission : obtain
   d. donation : refuse
   e. legacy : inherit

10. ADROIT : SKILLFUL : :
    a. juvenile : immature
    b. chaotic : disorganized
    c. musical : talented
    d. clumsy : awkward
    e. amateurish : unknown

11. MURDERER : CRUEL : :
    a. criminal : thief
    b. fugitive : hidden
    c. bully : mean
    d. killer : famous
    e. executioner : official

12. PUZZLE : UNDERSTAND : :
    a. confuse : comprehend
    b. consider : evaluate
    c. discover : conceal
    d. multiply : subtract
    e. suffer : enjoy

13. PAGEANT : PARADE : :
    a. sandwich : meal
    b. audience : mob
    c. rally : meeting
    d. concert : song
    e. battle : riot

14. MECHANIC : GARAGE : :
    a. stevedore : dock
    b. spectator : arena
    c. criminal : penitentiary
    d. engineer : plan
    e. biologist : microscope

15. FALTER : WALK : :
    a. lie : sleep
    b. stammer : speak
    c. glide : skate
    d. whirl : dance
    e. swallow : eat

16. CELEBRITY : FAMOUS : :
    a. hurricane : destructive
    b. president : elected
    c. artist : admired
    d. fugitive : pursued
    e. criminal : notorious

17. LOATHE : MONSTER : :
    a. venerate : hero
    b. tolerate : rascal
    c. dislike : job
    d. admire : scoundrel
    e. like : animals

18. INDICTMENT : LEGAL : :
    a. libel : untruthful
    b. charge : serious
    c. insult : vicious
    d. accusation : personal
    e. trial : official

19. CLERGYPERSON : PIOUS : :
    a. waiter : rude
    b. statue : stone
    c. warrior : martial
    d. receptionist : attractive
    e. writer : prolific

20. GARBAGE : PUTRID : :
    a. carriage : juvenile
    b. food : nutritious
    c. blotter : spotted
    d. weather : mild
    e. bouquet : fragrant

UNIT E

Directions: Circle the pair of words that most nearly expresses the relationship of the pair of key words in capital letters.

1. FATHER : SON : :
   a. grandparent : family
   b. brother : sister
   c. mother : daughter
   d. aunt : uncle
   e. family : city

2. ROOSTER : HEN : :
   a. bull : cow
   b. pony : horse
   c. cat : kitten
   d. whale : fish
   e. worm : snake

3. TASTY : FOOD : :
   a. liquid : milk
   b. red : apple
   c. dinner : meal
   d. fragrant : flower
   e. daily : sunshine

4. BOULDER : ROCK : :
   a. bay : cove
   b. mountain : hill
   c. pebble : stone
   d. sand : earth
   e. lion : cub

5. LAUNDRY : CLOTHES : :
   a. trunk : treasure
   b. beach : towels
   c. soap : hands
   d. cloth : car
   e. sink : dishes

6. ENTER : EXIT : :
   a. arrive : leave
   b. begin : continue
   c. start : stop
   d. door : open
   e. preliminary : secondary

7. ALCOHOLIC : DRINK : :
   a. romantic : dream
   b. glutton : eat
   c. motorist : drive
   d. fan : cheer
   e. pedestrian : walk

8. WARM : HOT : :
   a. boiling : warm
   b. ember : flame
   c. water : ice
   d. harsh : mile
   e. cool : cold

9. CELEBRATION : FESTIVE : :
   a. funeral : serious
   b. convention : organized
   c. party : joyful
   d. vacation : restful
   e. mob : unruly

10. EXCITED : CALM : :
    a. factual : opinionated
    b. aware : alert
    c. soothe : gentle
    d. rebellious : peaceful
    e. relaxed : silent

11. ACCOST : APPROACH : :
    a. deceive : betray
    b. delay : withhold
    c. import : deliver
    d. enter : walk
    e. desert : leave

12. PROVERB : WISDOM : :
    a. comma : punctuation
    b. slogan : business
    c. invitation : friendship
    d. pun : wit
    e. motto : words

13. MINUTES : MEETING : :
    a. lectures : school
    b. comments : debate
    c. notes : student
    d. calendar : events
    e. chronicle : history

14. BUSINESS : MANAGER : :
    a. band : leader
    b. movie : producer
    c. concert : musician
    d. symphony : conductor
    e. disco : dancer

15. CHECK : FACTS : :
    a. evaluate : information
    b. compile : statistics
    c. observe : details
    d. submit : report
    e. verify : truth

16. WORKER : PROFICIENT : :
    a. employee : honest
    b. craftswoman : adroit
    c. gymnast : spry
    d. authority : respected
    e. clerk : tolerant

17. RETARD : DEVELOPMENT : :
    a. develop : maturity
    b. withhold : information
    c. increase : speed
    d. overcome : opposition
    e. stunt : growth

18. TRAITOR : TREACHEROUS : :
    a. menace : evil
    b. coward : selfish
    c. umpire : fair
    d. liar : trustworthy
    e. confidant : hostile

19. PEER : EQUAL : :
    a. waiter : cheerful
    b. victor : triumphant
    c. classmate : classroom
    d. ambassador : elderly
    e. style : fashionable

20. EJECT : DISCARD : :
    a. accomplish : create
    b. maneuver : encircle
    c. endow : provide
    d. misplace : hide
    e. reject : retain

UNIT F

Directions: Circle the pair of words that most nearly expresses the relationship of the pair of key words in capital letters.

1. BANANA : YELLOW : :
   a. pear : sweet
   b. orange : sour
   c. purple : grape
   d. nut : hard
   e. apple : red

2. FAIR : GORGEOUS : :
   a. ugly : handsome
   b. pretty : beautiful
   c. wrestler : powerful
   d. cowgirl : brave
   e. unknown : famous

3. PAINTER : BRUSH : :
   a. author : pen
   b. teacher : book
   c. actor : stage
   d. musician : orchestra
   e. detective : badge

4. BOX : CRATE : :
   a. cigar : pipe
   b. table : floor
   c. cup : bowl
   d. market : customer
   e. cage : box

5. COMMERCIAL : TELEVISION : :
   a. page : book
   b. request : information
   c. station : radio
   d. communication : radio
   e. advertisement : newspaper

6. GARBAGE : CAN : :
   a. junk : attic
   b. water : pipe
   c. litter : basket
   d. groceries : cart
   e. milk : container

7. LAWN : GRASS : :
   a. forest : trees
   b. sea : Navy
   c. prairie : cattle
   d. valley : water
   e. avenue : people

8. GRAIN : SAND : :
   a. beach : ocean
   b. grass : ranch
   c. bowl : soup
   d. gallon : water
   e. drop : ink

9. MANIA : FRACTURE : :
   a. thoughtful : active
   b. hysterical : emotional
   c. injurious : healthful
   d. brain : heart
   e. mental : physical

10. EXTRICATE : DIFFICULTY : :
    a. complete : task
    b. refuse : offer
    c. consider : problem
    d. disentangle : knot
    e. abandon : hope

11. FORLORN : FROWN : :
    a. drowsy : sleep
    b. depressed : upset
    c. cheerful : smile
    d. optimistic : hope
    e. observant : see

12. MEMENTO : RECALL : :
    a. handbook : instruct
    b. diary : write
    c. date : celebrate
    d. souvenir : collect
    e. notes : remember

13. COERCE : CONVINCE : :
    a. compel : persuade
    b. follow : obey
    c. object : oppose
    d. charge : attack
    e. endorse : agree

14. OMIT : INCLUDE : :
    a. join : abandon
    b. reject : accept
    c. arrive : leave
    d. halt : start
    e. march : dance

15. POND : TRANQUIL : :
    a. sea : blue
    b. current : warm
    c. river : long
    d. whirlpool : swirling
    e. flood : wet

16. LENDER : DEBTOR : :
    a. donor : recipient
    b. author : reader
    c. teacher : student
    d. winner : loser
    e. executive : borrower

17. BAN : APPROVE : :
    a. prohibit : allow
    b. interpret : understand
    c. collide : hit
    d. worry : enjoy
    e. argue : agree

18. COURAGE : FEAR : :
    a. certainty : worry
    b. potency : weakness
    c. triumph : defeat
    d. confidence : uncertainty
    e. valor : cowardice

19. JEWEL : SHIMMER : :
    a. mirror : reflect
    b. fortune : accumulate
    c. fire : heat
    d. flame : flicker
    e. liquor : intoxicate

20. CREMATE : BODY : :
    a. attack : victim
    b. burn : house
    c. flood : basement
    d. kindle : fire
    e. admire : celebrity

UNIT G

Directions: Circle the pair of words that most nearly expresses the relationship of the pair of key words in capital letters.

1. TEACHER : SCHOOL : :
   a. doctor : patient
   b. author : book
   c. biologist : microscope
   d. soldier : battlefield
   e. surgeon : hospital

2. PEARL : NECKLACE : :
   a. car : train
   b. roof : house
   c. motor : automobile
   d. paper : wood
   e. point : pencil

3. COWARD : AFRAID : :
   a. artist : famous
   b. comedian : funny
   c. musician : athletic
   d. pupil : intelligent
   e. singer : loud

4. WATCH : TIME : :
   a. barometer : wind
   b. sundial : daylight
   c. atlas : maps
   d. calendar : date
   e. ruler : number

5. UNCLE SAM : UNITED STATES : :
   a. Robin Hood : archery
   b. Santa Claus : Christmas
   c. Lincoln : presidency
   d. baseball : sports
   e. Shakespeare : literature

6. IMPOSTER : DELUDE : :
   a. vandal : destroy
   b. spy : discover
   c. truant : hide
   d. swindler : deceive
   e. politician : exaggerate

7. DUSK : NIGHT : :
   a. twilight : day
   b. dawn : morning
   c. greetings : friendship
   d. start : race
   e. birth : life

8. CRIMSON : BLOUSE : :
   a. brown : trousers
   b. white : sneakers
   c. purple : ribbon
   d. formal : tuxedo
   e. red : shirt

9. ACCOMPLICE : AID : :
   a. ancestor : respect
   b. vandal : damage
   c. enemy : oppose
   d. friend : like
   e. relative : visit

10. PETITION : REQUEST : :
    a. advertisement : deception
    b. declaration : statement
    c. constitution : government
    d. ballot : vote
    e. document : diploma

11. PERTINENT : UNRELATED : :
    a. criminal : illegal
    b. corrupt : cruel
    c. deliberate : accidental
    d. disastrous : tragic
    e. dead : deceased

12. DECREPIT : HEALTHY : :
    a. attractive : ugly
    b. ancient : modern
    c. potent : powerful
    d. weak : strong
    e. enormous : small

13. SMART : INTELLIGENT : :
    a. mysterious : dark
    b. merry : gloomy
    c. polite : courteous
    d. ugly : beautiful
    e. certain : doubtful

14. HECTIC : CALM : :
    a. beautiful : plain
    b. talkative : mute
    c. active : frantic
    d. excited : relaxed
    e. primitive : modern

15. SHACK : FLIMSY : :
    a. tower : high
    b. chalet : snowy
    c. penthouse : high
    d. residence : comfortable
    e. castle : durable

16. DROUGHT : WATER : :
    a. famine : food
    b. credit : cash
    c. fog : sunlight
    d. diet : weight
    e. liquid : rain

17. START : BEGIN : :
    a. conclude : end
    b. erase : darken
    c. demand : shout
    d. transport : carry
    e. assemble : gather

18. EXPLICIT : UNCLEAR : :
    a. prosperous : poor
    b. abundant : scarce
    c. concealed : apparent
    d. confidential : truthful
    e. precise : vague

19. GENIAL : UNFRIENDLY : :
    a. cheerful : dour
    b. athletic : studious
    c. happy : contented
    d. pleasant : jolly
    e. courteous : rude

20. COLOSSAL : GIGANTIC : :
    a. floral : destructive
    b. devoted : related
    c. boisterous : noisy
    d. decisive : unsure
    e. essential : expensive

UNIT H

Directions: Circle the pair of words that most nearly expresses the relationship of the pair of key words in capital letters.

1. CARPENTER : HAMMER : :
   a. singer : song
   b. doctor : hospital
   c. judge : jury
   d. plumber : wrench
   e. soldier : rifle

2. TRUCK : CAR : :
   a. store : house
   b. string : rope
   c. yacht : lifeboat
   d. shirt : tie
   e. tower : hill

3. ATTACH : CONNECT : :
   a. destroy : ruin
   b. fasten : join
   c. gather : search
   d. assemble : talk
   e. participate : understand

4. SEARCH : EXPLORE : :
   a. glance : misjudge
   b. collect : save
   c. examine : inspect
   d. drive : travel
   e. overlook : forget

5. SENATOR : POLITICAL : :
   a. scholar : studious
   b. voter : national
   c. traveler : experienced
   d. executive : elderly
   e. gymnast : exceptional

6. STRADDLE : LEGS : :
   a. point : fingers
   b. work : muscles
   c. kneel : knees
   d. pat : palms
   e. embrace : arms

7. FRAUD : GENUINE : :
   a. answer : correct
   b. oath : legal
   c. deception : truthful
   d. mistake : significant
   e. defeat : victory

8. STARVATION : FOOD : :
   a. insomnia : sleep
   b. catastrophe : disaster
   c. bankruptcy : business
   d. water : thirst
   e. prairie : desert

9. BUD : BLOOM : :
   a. flower : smell
   b. twig : snap
   c. branch : break
   d. infant : grow
   e. river : flow

10. BENEFACTOR : GENEROUS : :
    a. miser : greedy
    b. expert : educated
    c. financier : trustworthy
    d. businesswoman : successful
    e. knight : brave

11. INNOVATION : TRADITION : :
    a. exciting : dull
    b. old : ancient
    c. different : same
    d. youth : age
    e. pittance : sad

12. WARFARE : CARNAGE : :
    a. examination : quiz
    b. contentment : peace
    c. precipitation : weather
    d. shadow : shade
    e. earthquake : destruction

13. PUNCH : FISTS : :
    a. stand : spine
    b. poke : fingers
    c. manicure : hands
    d. twist : ankles
    e. fracture : legs

14. ABHOR : DISLIKE : :
    a. automobile : truck
    b. tooth : mouth
    c. shoe : sandal
    d. feast : snack
    e. bag : carton

15. INCOMPREHENSIBLE : SPEECH : :
    a. illegible : writing
    b. meaningful : symbols
    c. insulting : remark
    d. inaccurate : statement
    e. incessant : sound

16. SEVER : DETACH : :
    a. change : shrink
    b. separate : remove
    c. cancel : deny
    d. commence : begin
    e. corrupt : destroy

17. EXPLANATION : CLEAR : :
    a. experience : historical
    b. puzzle : perplexing
    c. novel : lengthy
    d. riddle : brief
    e. outline : complete

18. DECREPIT : PERSON : :
    a. significant : event
    b. colorful : landscape
    c. pleasant : atmosphere
    d. religious : service
    e. ramshackle : house

19. DISDAIN : ACCEPTANCE : :
    a. resentment : approval
    b. competition : agreement
    c. reliance : faith
    d. scorn : hatred
    e. affection : devotion

20. LAWYER : CROSS EXAMINE : :
    a. inquisitor : question
    b. chef : congeal
    c. counsel : prosecute
    d. celebrity : autograph
    e. assistant : amplify

UNIT I

Directions: Circle the pair of words that most nearly expresses the relationship of the pair of key words in capital letters.

1. WINDOW : HOUSE : :
   a. crown : palace
   b. porthole : ship
   c. roof : cottage
   d. car : train
   e. glass : water

2. PENCIL : LEAD : :
   a. lighthouse : island
   b. pen : point
   c. torch : handle
   d. tree : branch
   e. candle : wick

3. SHRIEK : LOUD : :
   a. cry : voice
   b. snore : drowsy
   c. hum : monotonous
   d. whisper : soft
   e. chuckle : cheerful

4. DISAGREE : COMPLAIN : :
   a. differ : protest
   b. approve : agree
   c. talk : shout
   d. breathe : pant
   e. hate : dislike

5. BAG : PAPER : :
   a. sky : clouds
   b. garden : flowers
   c. snow : flakes
   d. carton : cardboard
   e. grass : hut

6. COLLEAGUE : PROFESSION : :
   a. manager : team
   b. captain : army
   c. co-worker : job
   d. boss : business
   e. janitor : factory

7. RELINQUISH : JOB : :
   a. spend : fortune
   b. abandon : position
   c. divorce : husband
   d. discontinue : habit
   e. job : quit

8. WEALTH : MANSION : :
   a. oblivion : cemetery
   b. strength : castle
   c. silence : chapel
   d. family : cottage
   e. poverty : shack

9. STICK : PLANK : :
   a. cigarette : cigar
   b. word : dictionary
   c. folder : envelope
   d. trunk : briefcase
   e. corridor : vestibule

10. SUMMIT : VALLEY : :
    a. peak : height
    b. high : low
    c. important : meaningless
    d. geranium : garden
    e. sound : silence

11. RECOMMEND : FRIEND : :
    a. suggest : idea
    b. fear : enemy
    c. endorse : product
    d. join : club
    e. respect : parent

12. EXPOSITION : FAIR : :
    a. airport : runway
    b. convention : meeting
    c. hotel : bungalow
    d. rally : race
    e. concert : song

13. LAMENT : SORROW : :
    a. cheer : approval
    b. handshake : support
    c. groan : excitement
    d. money : wealth
    e. weakness : illness

14. PREVAIL : STRUGGLE : :
    a. enjoy : competition
    b. win : award
    c. triumph : battle
    d. engage : conflict
    e. participate : match

15. DETOUR : DIVERT : :
    a. monument : remember
    b. injury : handicap
    c. barricade : halt
    d. fence : surround
    e. wall : construct

16. FINGER : HAND : :
    a. page : book
    b. roof : house
    c. tooth : mouth
    d. toe : foot
    e. button : shirt

17. INDIVIDUAL : POPULACE : :
    a. leader : crowd
    b. constitution : nation
    c. person : history
    d. victim : mob
    e. person : multitude

18. MEDAL : HONOR : :
    a. flag : nation
    b. badge : sheriff
    c. fame : achievement
    d. solace : defeat
    e. trophy : skill

19. SURPLUS : PLENTY : :
    a. paucity : few
    b. scarcity : none
    c. maximum : all
    d. minority : most
    e. quantity : some

20. FLIMSY : CONSTRUCTION : :
    a. vague : idea
    b. desperate : situation
    c. shoddy : work
    d. indelible : writing
    e. uncertain : attitude

UNIT J

Directions: Circle the pair of words that most nearly expresses the relationship of the pair of key words in capital letters.

1. ANT : INSECT : :
   a. pony : animal
   b. bird : eagle
   c. bee : fly
   d. dog : pet
   e. flower : rose

2. STORY : BOOK : :
   a. article : magazine
   b. version : newspaper
   c. page : textbook
   d. alphabet : letter
   e. item : list

3. CEASE : BEGIN : :
   a. close : open
   b. halt : finish
   c. open : close
   d. complete : start
   e. destroy : build

4. COMPLY : RULE : :
   a. consent : suggestion
   b. admit : error
   c. develop : interest
   d. approve : idea
   e. obey : regulation

5. ADVANCE : RETREAT : :
   a. walk : rest
   b. quarrel : argue
   c. proceed : withdraw
   d. accelerate : hurry
   e. promote : graduate

6. DISCARD : TRASH : :
   a. remove : waste
   b. accumulate : junk
   c. wash : dirt
   d. store : valuables
   e. correct : errors

7. OBSERVE : DEDUCE : :
   a. compare : purchase
   b. recall : remember
   c. inspect : conclude
   d. add : total
   e. consider : decide

8. EXPAND : SHRINK : :
   a. inflate : reduce
   b. narrow : widen
   c. build : construct
   d. organize : command
   e. catapult : hurl

9. LAW : NATION : :
   a. constitution : government
   b. regulation : business
   c. regulation : president
   d. rule : chairperson
   e. behavior : society

10. AMNESIA : MIND : :
    a. carnage : skin
    b. delight : heart
    c. oblivion : soul
    d. strength : health
    e. pneumonia : body

11. PONDER : ISSUE : :
    a. decide : suggestion
    b. consider : problem
    c. plan : campaign
    d. arrive : solution
    e. dream : success

12. MORAL : HONORABLE : :
    a. historic : glorious
    b. chic : fashionable
    c. filthy : awful
    d. chaste : pure
    e. helpful : desperate

13. UNPLEASANT : SMELL : :
    a. confident : feeling
    b. glorious : sight
    c. melodious : sound
    d. acrid : taste
    e. creative : mood

14. DEFEAT : SAD : :
    a. hike : tired
    b. tragedy : despondent
    c. victory : happy
    d. loss : exhausted
    e. game : excited

15. EXPAND : LARGE : :
    a. stretch : weak
    b. realize : clear
    c. contract : small
    d. review : important
    e. conceal : under

16. DETECT : DISCOVER : :
    a. accept : reject
    b. emphasize : shout
    c. find : conceal
    d. respect : condemn
    e. crave : desire

17. BAFFLE : PUZZLE : :
    a. soar : climb
    b. sprawl : stumble
    c. tile : lose
    d. stymie : obstruct
    e. discuss : contradict

18. CAMEL : DESERT : :
    a. typist : office
    b. animal : menagerie
    c. elephant : circus
    d. dog : kennel
    e. lion : jungle

19. CONCOCT : SCHEME : :
    a. construct : building
    b. paint : portrait
    c. devise : plan
    d. conceal : secret
    e. outline : essay

20. BELLOW : ROAR : :
    a. confiscate : possess
    b. confide : whisper
    c. discuss : speak
    d. shoot : injure
    e. clamor : shout

UNIT K

Directions: Circle the pair of words that most nearly expresses the relationship of the pair of key words in capital letters.

1. PRISON : JAIL : :
   a. cellar : tomb
   b. penitentiary : cell
   c. punishment : penalty
   d. convict : warden
   e. cellar : basement

2. MANAGER : EMPLOYEE : :
   a. company : corporation
   b. superintendent : school
   c. postmaster : mail carrier
   d. director : secretary
   e. warden : criminal

3. BIOGRAPHY : PERSON : :
   a. autobiography : celebrity
   b. history : nation
   c. geography : country
   d. geometry : mathematics
   e. narrative : story

4. HYPHEN : LINE : :
   a. apostrophe : omission
   b. number : amount
   c. parenthesis : circle
   d. period : dot
   e. comma : pause

5. PILLAR : COLUMN : :
   a. plank : board
   b. brick : pebble
   c. girder : steel
   d. soil : earth
   e. statue : painting

6. WRESTLER : MUSCULAR : :
   a. swimmer : liquid
   b. mountaineer : admirable
   c. boxer : skillful
   d. champion : famous
   e. basketball player : lanky

7. PAUSE : STRUGGLE : :
   a. intermission : play
   b. break : recess
   c. climax : battle
   d. touchdown : football game
   e. referee : prizefight

8. CLIQUE : FRIENDS : :
   a. building : rooms
   b. catalogue : cards
   c. team : opponents
   d. table : legs
   e. squad : soldiers

9. OBSERVE : EYE : :
   a. consider : mind
   b. lend : money
   c. reduce : weight
   d. notice : detail
   e. explore : courage

10. TOURIST : TRAVEL : :
    a. hitchhiker : wave
    b. consumer : purchase
    c. vagabond : reside
    d. nomad : wander
    e. champion : triumph

11. PROXIMITY : NEIGHBOR : :
    a. distance : foreigner
    b. patriotism : country
    c. devotion : parent
    d. cooperation : teammate
    e. fear : foe

12. DANGEROUS : SAFE : :
    a. healthy : wholesome
    b. honorable : dignified
    c. permanent : constant
    d. patient : calm
    e. imaginary : real

13. REPEAT : SPEECH : :
    a. sing : notes
    b. explain : letters
    c. request : writing
    d. duplicate : print
    e. add : numbers

14. SIGN : LETTER : :
    a. complete : task
    b. autograph : book
    c. insure : home
    d. write : message
    e. study : contract

15. LIAR : CANDOR : :
    a. forget : skill
    b. patriot : crime
    c. traitor : intelligence
    d. illiterate : learning
    e. cheater : honesty

16. WICK : BURN : :
    a. coal : heat
    b. mirror : reflect
    c. ember : smolder
    d. sunburn : irritate
    e. spotlight : shine

17. CATACLYSM : DISASTER : :
    a. earthquake : catastrophe
    b. bomb : explosion
    c. collision : destruction
    d. defeat : tragedy
    e. volcano : eruption

18. CROWD : GROUP : :
    a. army : squad
    b. store : market
    c. hospital : patient
    d. city : country
    e. election : candidate

19. HARASS : DISTURB : :
    a. justify : decide
    b. inhibit : hold back
    c. repair : adjust
    d. validate : stamp
    e. specialize : improve

20. FOOD : CONTAMINATED : :
    a. soil : sandy
    b. air : healthful
    c. water : polluted
    d. blood : red
    e. fire : hot

UNIT L

Directions: Circle the pair of words that most nearly expresses the relationship of the pair of key words in capital letters.

1. BATTLESHIP : WARFARE : :
   a. canoe : exploration
   b. yacht : pleasure
   c. rowboat : exercise
   d. sailboat : competition
   e. raft : adventure

2. PARAGRAPH : PAGE : :
   a. note : melody
   b. sentence : story
   c. letter : word
   d. telegram : message
   e. memorandum : sheet of paper

3. RADIO : COMMERCIAL : :
   a. book : page
   b. magazine : article
   c. cassette : sound
   d. newspaper : advertisement
   e. television : announcer

4. WAR : ARMISTICE : :
   a. battle : struggle
   b. divorce : marriage
   c. peace : treaty
   d. dispute : settlement
   e. argument : debate

5. BUS : AUTOMOBILE : :
   a. house : hotel
   b. cat : mouse
   c. college : school
   d. mall : store
   e. afraid : frighten

6. DINGY : DARK : :
   a. rainy : dry
   b. obedient : cooperative
   c. damp : moist
   d. courageous : brave
   e. afraid : frightened

7. REMIT : PAYMENT : :
   a. cancel : debt
   b. write : letter
   c. save : dollar
   d. appreciate : favor
   e. mail : check

8. TRINKET : CHEAP : :
   a. gem : expensive
   b. bond : financial
   c. money : legal
   d. gadget : useful
   e. gold : wealthy

9. TRIBUTARY : RIVER : :
   a. office : corporation
   b. table : rug
   c. pearl : necklace
   d. state : nation
   e. branch : tree

10. ACCUMULATE : COLLECT : :
    a. insure : protect
    b. distribute : give
    c. invest : profit
    d. plan : design
    e. develop : disintegrate

11. SUMMARY : STORY : :
    a. slice : pie
    b. sample : product
    c. abbreviation : word
    d. resumé : career
    e. song : concert

12. MEMORANDUM : BREVITY : :
    a. notebook : details
    b. telegram : eminent
    c. epic : length
    d. letter : information
    e. novel : characters

13. CARTOON : DRAWING : :
    a. ruby : gem
    b. picture : album
    c. snapshot : photograph
    d. painting : masterpiece
    e. camera : instrument

14. GARDEN : FRAGRANCE : :
    a. nostril : smell
    b. lawn : grass
    c. kitchen : aroma
    d. cellar : darkness
    e. roof : sunlight

15. MERRY : CHEERFUL : :
    a. garrulous : talkative
    b. aware : forgetful
    c. joyful : youthful
    d. shrewd : honest
    e. soothing : irritable

16. RETARD : DELAY : :
    a. shatter : break
    b. strain : struggle
    c. advance : improve
    d. repel : drive back
    e. imprison : free

17. SWAMP : SULTRY : :
    a. farm : agricultural
    b. glacier : frigid
    c. plateau : flat
    d. horizon : visionary
    e. igloo : inhabited

18. GUARD : ALERT : :
    a. monitor : strict
    b. author : popular
    c. economist : scientific
    d. majorette : acrobatic
    e. watchman : vigilant

19. ESCALATE : DIMINISH : :
    a. increase : dwindle
    b. inform : educate
    c. organize : strengthen
    d. infect : poison
    e. spend : save

20. VALLEY : LOW : :
    a. oval : circular
    b. tumult : steep
    c. pinnacle : high
    d. lawn : green
    e. lake : shallow

UNIT M

Directions: Circle the pair of words that most nearly expresses the relationship of the pair of key words in capital letters.

1. BUTTON : SHIRT : :
   a. tie : neck
   b. wheel : wagon
   c. driver : motorcycle
   d. eyeglasses : nose
   e. lace : shoe

2. SAILOR : CREW : :
   a. conductor : orchestra
   b. actor : drama
   c. guest : party
   d. player : team
   e. pupil : school

3. LIZARD : DRAGON : :
   a. bungalow : castle
   b. whale : fish
   c. soldier : general
   d. leaf : vine
   e. pigeon : eagle

4. PARENT : ALLOW : :
   a. judge : deny
   b. friend : encourage
   c. sovereign : tolerate
   d. opponent : prevent
   e. principal : permit

5. HISTORY : NATION : :
   a. biography : person
   b. geography : continent
   c. photography : person
   d. artillery : army
   e. constitution : country

6. CARPENTRY : BOARDS : :
   a. masonry : bricks
   b. archery : arrows
   c. biology : microscopes
   d. poetry : rhymes
   e. geography : maps

7. ARGUMENT : BRAWL : :
   a. revolt : battle
   b. challenge : struggle
   c. debate : fight
   d. insult : hatred
   e. tension : conflict

8. BEGGAR : DESTITUTE : :
   a. investor : cautious
   b. model : beautiful
   c. taxpayer : financial
   d. millionaire : wealthy
   e. victim : pitiful

9. ANNOY : EXASPERATE : :
   a. memorize : repeat
   b. charm : fascinate
   c. save : invest
   d. devastate : harm
   e. grow : dwindle

10. BUCCANEER : SHIP : :
    a. burglar : house
    b. servant : palace
    c. trespasser : lawn
    d. thief : jewels
    e. pirate : treasure

11. WRATH : ENEMY : :
    a. respect : opponent
    b. pride : country
    c. belief : myth
    d. loyalty : cause
    e. affection : friend

12. LYRICAL : JOY : :
    a. contented : happiness
    b. tortured : pain
    c. mournful : sadness
    d. discouraged : failure
    e. dry : thirsty

13. PROXIMITY : NEAR : :
    a. truthful : valid
    b. ancient : old
    c. adjacent : friendly
    d. distance : far
    e. decisive : significant

14. COLOSSUS : HUGE : :
    a. dress : fashionable
    b. germ : microscopic
    c. majority : large
    d. iota : small
    e. archer : accurate

15. SILVER : TARNISH : :
    a. gold : shine
    b. gem : sparkle
    c. paper : write
    d. metal : rust
    e. fire : singe

16. REVERE : MOCK : :
    a. admire : regard
    b. pray : chatter
    c. respect : scoff
    d. detest : praise
    e. plan : succeed

17. REBUT : AGREE : :
    a. confirm : justify
    b. reduce : lessen
    c. develop : expand
    d. acknowledge : recognize
    e. contradict : approve

18. BUSINESS : DEFUNCT : :
    a. corporation : bankrupt
    b. enthusiasm : diminished
    c. meeting : concluded
    d. weight : reduced
    e. vacation : extended

19. DEPARTURE : EXODUS : :
    a. excitement : commotion
    b. meeting : celebration
    c. arrival : welcome
    d. farewell : journey
    e. arrival : influx

20. ARBITRATOR : DECISION : :
    a. court : ruling
    b. company : agreement
    c. debtor : contract
    d. bookkeeper : total
    e. surgeon : dissection

UNIT N

Directions: Circle the pair of words that most nearly expresses the relationship of the pair of key words in capital letters.

1. BANANA : FRUIT : :
   a. grape : sweet
   b. balloon : toy
   c. onion : round
   d. tomato : vegetable
   e. coconut : hard

2. DINOSAUR : BIG : :
   a. caterpillar : round
   b. butterfly : beautiful
   c. lizard : small
   d. dot : tiny
   e. rabbit : furry

3. CAR : FACTORY : :
   a. skate : rink
   b. shop : jeans
   c. radio : store
   d. cake : bakery
   e. fire : furnace

4. LEARN : CLASS : :
   a. exercise : gym
   b. erect : tent
   c. attend : school
   d. join : organization
   e. win : ring

5. CARTOON : PICTURE : :
   a. book : encyclopedia
   b. hymn : song
   c. food : hamburger
   d. valley : mountain
   e. jet : plane

6. BOMB : EXPLODE : :
   a. current : flow
   b. wheel : spin
   c. drizzle : fall
   d. bus : transport
   e. volcano : erupt

7. CART : WAGON : :
   a. cot : bed
   b. pencil : pen
   c. boot : sneaker
   d. meal : snack
   e. paper : cardboard

8. BLEAK : CHEERFUL : :
   a. cold : snowy
   b. bare : flat
   c. bold : brave
   d. gloomy : pleasant
   e. bright : dark

9. CARELESSNESS : MISHAP : :
   a. thrift : poverty
   b. legislation : law
   c. disease : death
   d. worry : depression
   e. oversight : error

10. SYNOPSIS : BOOK : :
    a. outline : index
    b. summary : story
    c. paragraph : page
    d. slice : pie
    e. chemical : formula

11. EDUCATED : PROFESSOR : :
    a. large : university
    b. strict : principal
    c. intelligent : scholar
    d. difficult : textbook
    e. attentive : pupil

12. RENDEZVOUS : FRIENDS : :
    a. devotion : family
    b. competition : rivals
    c. business : customer
    d. obedience : parents
    e. clash : enemies

13. IMMINENT : SOON : :
    a. preferred : desirable
    b. regardless : neglectful
    c. ignorant : experienced
    d. eventually : later
    e. finally : decisive

14. DRIP : SEEP : :
    a. leak : ooze
    b. wave : ripple
    c. pour : spill
    d. current : stream
    e. flood : wash

15. REGRET : ERROR : :
    a. overlook : mistake
    b. publicity : crime
    c. impatience : evil
    d. rejection : friendship
    e. sorrow : sin

16. IMPROVE : AGGRAVATE : :
    a. circular : square
    b. better : worse
    c. cement : asphalt
    d. hazy : sunny
    e. collect : distribute

17. INQUEST : INVESTIGATION : :
    a. charge : conviction
    b. term : semester
    c. judge : lawyer
    d. larceny : crime
    e. court martial : trial

18. TURMOIL : TROUBLE : :
    a. suspicion : doubt
    b. silence : speech
    c. movement : travel
    d. instruction : learning
    e. acceptance : charity

19. ABHOR : ENEMY : :
    a. enjoy : treat
    b. regret : error
    c. adore : hero
    d. worship : church
    e. obey : conqueror

20. ABANDON : LEAVE : :
    a. brandish : conceal
    b. edit : revise
    c. heed : obey
    d. blunder : regret
    e. depart : desert

UNIT O

Directions : Circle the pair of words that most nearly expresses the relationship of the pair of key words in capital letters.

1. FEMALE : WOMAN : :
   a. male : man
   b. fish : shark
   c. palace : house
   d. girl : human
   e. tiger : animal

2. ILLNESS : HEALTH : :
   a. weakness : strength
   b. sickness : disease
   c. young : old
   d. wood : brick
   e. ignorance : knowledge

3. RULE : OBEY : :
   a. pirate : ocean
   b. order : follow
   c. guide : tourist
   d. police officer : law
   e. sovereign : subject

4. FOOTBALL : FIELD : :
   a. baseball : team
   b. basketball : hoop
   c. hockey : winter
   d. tennis : court
   e. sports : stadium

5. BARBER : HAIR : :
   a. librarian : school
   b. dentist : teeth
   c. tailor : thread
   d. doctor : health
   e. lawyer : case

6. FROG : HOP : :
   a. beaver : work
   b. snake : glide
   c. bear : bite
   d. camel : drink
   e. wriggle : worm

7. UNDAUNTED : EXPLORER : :
   a. admired : astronaut
   b. famous : champion
   c. fearless : adventurer
   d. powerful : boxer
   e. experienced : pilot

8. AFFECTION : FRIEND : :
   a. rancor : foe
   b. opposition : enemy
   c. devotion : cause
   d. preference : choice
   e. envy : celebrity

9. COMEDY : AMUSING : :
   a. drama : hilarious
   b. story : serious
   c. biography : informative
   d. sketch : brief
   e. musical : songs

10. CHIC : ATTIRE : :
    a. powerful : effects
    b. denim : jeans
    c. popular : personalities
    d. fashionable : clothes
    e. critical : reviews

11. COPIOUS : NOTES : :
    a. plentiful : details
    b. significant : facts
    c. important : dates
    d. valuable : gifts
    e. accurate : records

12. PROFITABLE : BUSINESS : :
    a. significant : event
    b. unkept : promise
    c. formal : introduction
    d. responsible : position
    e. lucrative : job

13. PITTANCE : FORTUNE : :
    a. butter : bread
    b. crumb : loaf
    c. storm : rainfall
    d. silver : coin
    e. teller : bank

14. JEST : JOKE : :
    a. play : comedy
    b. pun : word
    c. smile : chuckle
    d. prank : trick
    e. comedian : entertainer

15. ILLEGIBLE : SCRIBBLE : :
    a. improved : develop
    b. colorful : paint
    c. incoherent : mumble
    d. athletic : compete
    e. prohibited : violate

16. REPLENISH : SUPPLY : :
    a. reinforce : safe
    b. divide : portion
    c. accumulate : wealth
    d. achieve : majority
    e. refill : glass

17. PAINTER : BRUSH : :
    a. golfer : course
    b. jogger : energy
    c. gardener : rake
    d. postman : stamp
    e. farmer : hay

18. TRIP : JOURNEY : :
    a. conjecture : meeting
    b. cavalcade : tour
    c. marathon : race
    d. picnic : party
    e. cruise : voyage

19. PENSIVE : THOUGHTFUL : :
    a. careless : forgetful
    b. destitute : certain
    c. proficient : convincing
    d. plausible : reasonable
    e. intelligent : studious

20. INQUISITIVE : QUESTIONS : :
    a. religious : prayers
    b. daring : experiences
    c. definite : statements
    d. undaunted : adventures
    e. curious : observations

VOCABULARY GROUP I

1. **accost**—*(v.)* to approach and speak to another person, often in a challenging way.

2. **accusation**—*(n.)* a charge of guilt or blame.

3. **adroit**—*(adj.)* skillful; expert in use of the hands or mind.

4. **alias**—*(n.)* an assumed name.

5. **amendment**—*(n.)* an addition or change, usually to a law or regulation.

6. **apathy**—*(n.)* a lack of interest, indifference.

7. **assert**—*(v.)* to state strongly.

8. **beacon**—*(n.)* a light for warning or guiding.

9. **beneficiary**—*(n.)* one who receives benefits; one who receives gifts.

10. **betray**—*(v.)* to deceive; to act like a traitor.

11. **blunder**—*(n.)* a stupid mistake.

12. **caddie**—*(n.)* a person who carries a player's golf clubs.

13. **chronicle**—*(n.)* a year by year record of historical events in the order of time.

14. **compile**—*(v.)* to collect and bring together in one list or account.

15. **concur**—*(v.)* to agree; to be of the same opinion.

16. **confidant**—*(n.)* a close friend trusted with secret or private affairs.

17. **congregation**—*(n.)* a group of people who worship in a church, synagogue, or other religious institution.

18. **conjecture**—*(n.)* the formation of an opinion without proof.—*(v.)* to conclude from insufficient evidence.

19. **connoisseur**—*(n.)* someone who can competently judge fine art.

20. **consumer**—*(n.)* a customer; one who buys a product.

21. **contour**—*(n.)* the outline or shape of a figure or body.

22. **contradict**—*(v.)* to assert the opposite.

23. **counterfeit**—*(n.)* a phony imitation.—*(v.)* to imitate in order to deceive.

24. **cult**—*(n.)* a small, often unusual, religious group.

25. **decade**—*(n.)* a period of ten years.

26. **defendant**—*(n.)* a person accused or sued in a law court.

27. **dietician**—*(n.)* a person who is trained to plan meals according to nutritional rules.

28. **donor**—*(n.)* a person who gives or donates.

29. **efficient**—*(adj.)* working well, effectively, and without waste.

30. **eject**—*(v.)* to drive out or force out; to dismiss.

31. **encore**—*(n.)* something done again because of a special request; an extra musical selection.

32. **endow**—*(v.)* to provide with a permanent fund or source of income.

33. **erroneous**—*(adj.)* mistaken; incorrect.

34. **evacuate**—*(v.)* to leave a place quickly, as in an emergency.

35. **falter**—*(v.)* to hesitate or waver; to become unsteady.

36. **fertile**—*(adj.)* productive; able to bear seeds, fruits, or vegetables.

37. **feud**—*(n.)* a long lasting dispute between families or other groups.

38. **fickle**—*(adj.)* likely to change without reason; unstable.

39. **foretell**—*(v.)* to tell in advance; to predict the future.

40. **fugitive**—*(n.)* a person who is fleeing or has fled, especially from the law.

41. **garrison**—*(n.)* a group of soldiers stationed in a fortified place.

42. **glutton**—*(n.)* one who indulges in something excessively, especially food; an overeater.

43. **gullible**—*(adj.)* easily fooled or deceived.

44. **haphazard**—*(adj.)* marked by lack of plan, order, or direction.

45. **hermit**—*(n.)* a person who lives alone, or away from people.

46. **hostile**—*(adj.)* unfriendly; warlike.

47. **illicit**—*(adj.)* not permitted by law; forbidden; improper.

48. **inaugurate**—*(v.)* to install into public office with a ceremony.

49. **indictment**—*(n.)* an accusation; in law, a formal accusation by a grand jury.

50. **initiate**—*(v.)* to begin; to admit with a ceremony to a group or an organization; to set going.—*(n.)* one who has been initiated or admitted.

51. **invigorate**—*(v.)* to refresh, to give new strength.

52. **irate**—*(adj.)* very angry; furious.

53. **jeer**—*(v.)* to make fun of rudely or unkindly; ridicule.

54. **legacy**—*(n.)* a gift of property, especially by a legal will.

55. **loathe**—*(v.)* to feel hatred, disgust, or intense dislike.

56. **marathon**—*(n.)* a foot race of about 26 miles; any long race or contest.

57. **martial**—*(adj.)* warlike; inclined to fighting.

58. **menace**—*(n.)* someone who threatens to cause harm or evil.—*(v.)* to threaten.

59. **morbid**—*(adj.)* gloomy or unwholesome; sickly; relating to a disease.

60. **mutiny**—*(n.)* a revolt against authority, usually by soldiers or sailors.

61. **notorious**—*(adj.)* widely but unfavorably known.

62. **odyssey**—*(n.)* any journey filled with wandering.

63. **pageant**—*(n.)* an elaborate public spectacle or ceremonial parade.

64. **peer**—*(n.)* an equal; a person of the same age or rank as another.

65. **penitentiary**—*(n.)* a large prison or jail.

66. **peruse**—*(v.)* to read thoroughly and carefully.

67. **pilfer**—*(v.)* to steal, especially in small quantities; to snatch.

68. **pious**—*(adj.)* religious; devoted to a religious life.

69. **pitfall**—*(n.)* a trap; a concealed pit prepared as a trap for animals or people.

70. **preliminary**—*(adj.)* something coming before the main business; introductory.

71. **prelude**—*(n.)* anything serving as an introduction; a short piece of music before a concert.

72. **proficient**—*(adj.)* skilled; expert in an art, science, or subject.

73. **prolific**—*(adj.)* extremely productive or fruitful.

74. **proverb**—*(n.)* a short, wise saying used for a long time by many people.

75. **pun**—*(n.)* a humorous play on words with the words having the same sound but different meanings.

76. **putrid**—*(adj.)* rotten; foul; stinking.

77. **ramble**—*(v.)* to wander; to talk or write without a sequence of ideas.

78. **rebut**—*(v.)* try to disprove; to oppose by evidence on the other side of an argument.

79. **reminisce**—*(v.)* to recall past experiences.

80. **remnant**—*(n.)* a small part or quantity remaining; a trace.

81. **replica**—*(n.)* a copy or reproduction.

82. **retard**—*(v.)* to slow something down; to delay progress; to hold back; to hinder.

83. **robust**—*(adj.)* strong and healthy; sturdy.

84. **scroll**—*(n.)* a roll of paper or parchment with writing on it.

85. **scoundrel**—*(n.)* a villain; a deceptive and dishonest person.

86. **sedate**—*(adj.)* quiet; calm; serious.

87. **sever**—*(v.)* to cut apart; to separate.

88. **squad**—*(n.)* a small group; an athletic team or military unit.

89. **stevedore**—*(n.)* a worker who unloads cargo from a ship.

90. **submit**—*(v.)* to yield; to give in to; to surrender.

91. **surmount**—*(v.)* to overcome; to get over.

92. **terminate**—*(v.)* to put an end to; to end.

93. **traitor**—*(n.)* a person who betrays a friend, a duty, or his or her country.

94. **triumphant**—*(adj.)* victorious; successful.

95. **uncouth**—*(adj.)* awkward or clumsy in shape or appearance; crude in manners; unmannerly.

96. **unruly**—*(adj.)* unable to be controlled.

97. **utensil**—*(n.)* an instrument or implement, especially for use in the kitchen.

98. **vehement**—*(adj.)* forceful; showing strong feeling.

99. **venerate**—*(v.)* regard with great respect.

100. **verify**—*(v.)* to prove to be true; to confirm.

VOCABULARY GROUP II

1. **abhor**—(v.) to hate, to loathe.

2. **accelerate**—(v.) to speed up, to move faster.

3. **accomplice**—(n.) a partner in crime.

4. **acrid**—(adj.) sharp or biting in taste; bitter.

5. **amnesia**—(n.) loss of memory.

6. **amplify**—(v.) to make greater, stronger, or larger.

7. **baffle**—(v.) to puzzle.

8. **ban**—(v.) to prohibit or forbid.

9. **bellow**—(v.) to roar; to make a hollow, loud cry.

10. **benefactor**—(n.) a kindly helper; one who gives a gift.

11. **boisterous**—(adj.) rough and noisy; stormy.

12. **carnage**—(n.) the slaughter of a great number of people; destruction; a massacre.

13. **catapult**—(n.) an ancient military weapon for throwing large stones; a modern device for launching an airplane from a ship's deck.—(v.) to shoot from a catapult.

14. **cease**—(v.) to stop, end, or discontinue.

15. **chaste**—(adj.) pure in character; pure in taste or style.

16. **chic**—(adj.) fashionable, stylish, attractive.

17. **clamor**—(n.) a loud noise; an uproar.

18. **coerce**—(v.) to force or compel.

19. **colleague**—(n.) an associate; a co-worker in a profession.

20. **colossal**—(adj.) gigantic, huge, vast.

21. **commence**—(v.) to begin or start.

22. **compel**—(v.) to force to a course of action; to bring about by force.

23. **comply**—(v.) to act in agreement with.

24. **concoct**—(v.) to make by combining ingredients.

25. **confide**—(v.) to tell as a secret; to put trust in.

26. **confiscate**—(v.) to seize by legal authority.

27. **congeal**—(v.) to change from a fluid to a solid state; to thicken.

28. **cowardice**—(n.) lack of courage.

29. **crave**—(v.) to desire strongly.

30. **cremate**—(v.) to reduce a corpse to ashes; to consume by fire.

31. **crimson**—(adj.) deep, purplish red.

32. **debtor**—(n.) one who owes money; one who is in debt.

33. **deception**—(n.) a lie; the act of making something that is not true seem to be true.

34. **decrepit**—(adj.) weakened by old age; feeble; infirm.

35. **deduce**—(v.) to come to a conclusion based on something known or assumed.

36. **delude**—(v.) to mislead; to deceive.

37. **despondent**—(adj.) very sad; depressed; dejected.

38. **detach**—(v.) to unfasten and separate; to disunite.

39. **detect**—(v.) to discover the presence, existence or fact of.

40. **devise**—(v.) to form a plan in one's mind by combining ideas; to create.

41. **disdain**—(v.) to hate, to despise; to scorn.—(n.) contempt or scorn.

42. **divert**—(v.) to turn from one thing to another; to turn one's attention away from something, especially through entertainment.

43. **dour**—(adj.) sullen, gloomy in manner.

44. **drought**—(n.) the absence of rain; dry weather.

45. **durable**—(adj.) lasting, enduring.

46. **endorse**—(v.) to approve; to support; to write your name on the back of a check.

47. **engage**—(v.) to involve; to keep busy; to hire; to promise to marry.

48. **explicit**—(adj.) clearly expressed.

49. **exposition**—(n.) a large public exhibition or show; an explanation.

50. **extricate**—(v.) to disentangle.

51. **famine**—(n.) extreme and general scarcity of food; extreme hunger, starvation.

52. **forlorn**—(adj.) abandoned; sad and lonely because of isolation.

53. **fraud**—(n.) dishonesty; deception.

54. **genial**—(adj.) cheerful; cordial; lively.

55. **imposter**—(n.) a person who pretends to be another person; a fraud.

56. **incessant**—(adj.) ceaseless; continuing without interruption.

57. **indelible**—(adj.) incapable of being erased.

58. **innovation**—(n.) something new.

59. **inquisitor**—(n.) a harsh, merciless questioner.

60. **insomnia**—(n.) inability to sleep; sleeplessness.

61. **intoxicate**—(v.) to make drunk; to excite beyond control.

62. **lament**—(v.) to express grief or sorrow.—(n.) an expression of grief or sorrow.

63. **litter**—(n.) trash, waste, or garbage scattered about.—(v.) to scatter.

64. **mania**—(n.) a psychological condition characterized by unreasonable excitement.

65. **memento**—(n.) a reminder; a souvenir.

66. **menagerie**—(n.) a collection of animals.

67. **mute**—(adj.) silent.—(n.) a person who is unable to speak.

68. **oblivion**—(n.) the state of being forgotten.

69. **omit**—(v.) to leave out.

70. **paucity**—(n.) scantiness; fewness; smallness of quantity.

71. **penthouse**—(n.) an apartment built on a roof, usually on a high building.

72. **perplex**—(v.) to confuse, bewilder, or puzzle.

73. **pertinent**—(adj.) relevant; pertaining to the matter at hand.

74. **petition**—(n.) a formal written request addressed to authorities requesting a right, favor or other benefit.—(v.) to request formally.

75. **pittance**—(n.) a very small amount of something like money.

76. **ponder**—(v.) to consider carefully; to meditate.

77. **populace**—(n.) the people of a community or nation.

78. **potent**—(adj.) powerful; very strong; highly effective.

79. **precipitation**—(n.) natural matter such as snow or rain which falls from the sky.

80. **precise**—(adj.) definite, exact, strictly stated.

81. **prevail**—(v.) to predominate or conquer; to be superior in strength, power, or influence.

82. **primitive**—(adj.) simple, crude; ancient; characterized by an early stage of development.

83. **prohibit**—(v.) to forbid, prevent, or hinder.

84. **ramshackle**—(adj.) rickety, shaky, loosely made or held together.

85. **recipient**—(n.) a person or group that receives something.

86. **reliance**—(n.) dependence upon; trust.

87. **relinquish**—(v.) to give up; to let go.

88. **scorn**—(n.) open contempt; mockery.

89. **shimmer**—(v.) to shine with a sparkling light.

90. **shoddy**—(adj.) anything that is inferior but made to appear better; flimsy.

91. **solace**—(n.) comfort in sorrow or trouble; consolation.

92. **stigma**—(n.) a mark of disgrace or shame.

93. **straddle**—(v.) to stand or sit with the legs wide apart, especially with a leg on each side of something like a horse, bicycle, chair, ditch, etc.

94. **stymie**—(v.) to hinder; to block.

95. **summit**—(n.) the highest point.

96. **surplus**—(n.) an extra amount of something; an excess.

97. **tranquil**—(adj.) quiet; calm, peaceful, undisturbed.

98. **truant**—(n.) one who is absent without permission, usually from school.

99. **valor**—(n.) bravery, courage.

100. **vestibule**—(n.) a passage, a hall, or a small room at the entrance of a building.

VOCABULARY GROUP III

1. **accumulate**—*(v.)* to heap up; to gather or collect.

2. **adjacent**—*(adj.)* nearby; next to.

3. **aggravate**—*(v.)* to intensify; to make worse; to irritate.

4. **arbitrator**—*(n.)* a person chosen to settle a dispute.

5. **armistice**—*(n.)* a truce; a temporary declaration of peace.

6. **autobiography**—*(n.)* a book written by a person about his/her life.

7. **biography**—*(n.)* a book about the life of a person written by another person.

8. **bleak**—*(adj.)* bare, dreary.

9. **brandish**—*(v.)* to shake or wave, as with a weapon.

10. **brevity**—*(n.)* the quality of being brief.

11. **buccaneer**—*(n.)* a pirate.

12. **candor**—*(n.)* fairness; honesty, frankness.

13. **cataclysm**—*(n.)* a sudden violent change in the earth's surface; an extensive flood.

14. **cavalcade**—*(n.)* a procession or long parade, especially of people on horseback.

15. **clique**—*(n.)* a small group of people with similar interests.

16. **colossus**—*(n.)* a huge statue; anything huge or gigantic.

17. **confirm**—*(v.)* to make certain or verify; admit to full membership in a church.

18. **contaminate**—*(v.)* to make impure by contact or mixture.

19. **copious**—*(adj.)* large in quantity or number; abundant.

20. **corporation**—*(n.)* an association of people organized by law to act as a business.

21. **critical**—*(adj.)* inclined to find fault.

22. **defunct**—*(adj.)* dead, deceased; extinct.

23. **destitute**—*(adj.)* lacking means or resources; deprived; penniless.

24. **dignified**—*(adj.)* respectable, stately, noble.

25. **dingy**—*(adj.)* dark, dull, or dirty.

26. **disintegrate**—*(v.)* to break up; to separate into small parts.

27. **dispute**—*(n.)* an argument, quarrel, or difference of opinion.

28. **dissection**—*(n.)* a process of cutting apart.

29. **duplicate**—*(n.)* an exact copy.—*(v.)* to copy or reproduce exactly.

30. **dwindle**—*(v.)* to become smaller or to shrink.

31. **edit**—*(v.)* to prepare for publication; to change something like writing for the purpose of improving it.

32. **eminent**—*(adj.)* standing out and easily noticed; above all others especially in terms of a particular quality; distinguished.

33. **epic**—*(n.)* a long poem that tells of the adventures of a great hero.

34. **erupt**—*(v.)* to burst forth or explode.

35. **escalate**—*(v.)* to increase gradually; to ascend or rise.

36. **exasperate**—*(v.)* to irritate intensely; to annoy extremely; to infuriate.

37. **exodus**—*(n.)* a departure by many people.

38. **garrulous**—*(adj.)* talkative.

39. **girder**—*(n.)* a horizontal building support, usually made of steel or iron.

40. **harass**—*(v.)* to trouble by repeated attacks; to disturb; to torment.

41. **heed**—*(v.)* to give attention to; to notice; to obey.

42. **illegible**—*(adj.)* incapable of being read.

43. **illiterate**—*(n.)* a person who is unable to read or write.—*(adj.)* unable to read or write.

44. **imminent**—*(adj.)* likely to occur at any moment.

45. **incoherent**—*(adj.)* difficult to understand; mixed up.

46. **index**—*(n.)* an alphabetical listing of the items—topics, names, etc.—in a book, and the pages on which to find them.

47. **influx**—*(n.)* a flowing in.

48. **inhibit**—*(v.)* to restrain, hinder, or hold back.

49. **inquest**—*(n.)* a legal inquiry before a jury; an investigation.

50. **inquisitive**—*(adj.)* curious; asking many questions.

51. **iota**—*(n.)* a small quantity; a jot.

52. **justify**—*(v.)* to prove as being correct; to make excuses for.

53. **lanky**—*(adj.)* ungracefully tall and thin.

54. **larceny**—*(n.)* the act of stealing; theft.

55. **lucrative**—*(adj.)* profitable; producing wealth.

56. **lyrical**—*(adj.)* expressing strong emotion, particularly joyous emotion.

57. **masonry**—*(n.)* stonework; brickwork; the trade of a person who builds by using units of material like stone or brick.

58. **memorandum**—*(n.)* a brief note or reminder.

59. **mishap**—*(n.)* an unfortunate accident.

60. **narrative**—*(n.)* a story or tale.

61. **nomad**—*(n.)* a wanderer; one of a tribe that moves from place to place.

62. **omission**—*(n.)* something left out.

63. **pact**—*(n.)* an agreement; a treaty.

64. **patriot**—*(n.)* a person faithful to his or her country.

65. **pensive**—*(adj.)* deeply and seriously thoughtful.

66. **pillar**—*(n.)* an upright column, usually made of stone and often used to support a building.

67. **pinnacle**—*(n.)* the highest point; a lofty peak.

68. **plausible**—*(adj.)* reasonable; having the appearance of truth.

69. **porous**—*(adj.)* full of pores or tiny holes

70. **proximity**—*(n.)* nearness in place, time, or relationship.

71. **rancor**—*(n.)* bitter resentment; hatred.

72. **reinforce**—*(v.)* to strengthen, to make more powerful.

73. **remit**—*(v.)* to send money.

74. **rendezvous**—*(n.)* an appointed place for a meeting.—*(v.)* to meet at a particular place.

75. **repel**—*(v.)* to drive back; to resist by fighting against.

76. **replenish**—*(v.)* to supply fully; to restore to completeness.

77. **resumé**—*(n.)* a summary of a person's qualifications or career experience.

78. **revere**—*(v.)* to look upon with respect and awe.

79. **scoff**—*(v.)* to ridicule; to mock.

80. **seep**—*(v.)* to leak out; to pass gradually through a porous surface.

81. **shrewd**—*(adj.)* clever or smart in a tricky way.

82. **significant**—*(adj.)* very important.

83. **singe**—*(v.)* to burn slightly.—*(n.)* a slight burn.

84. **smolder**—*(v.)* to burn or smoke without flame.

85. **sovereign**—*(n.)* a ruler like a king or a queen.

86. **subject**—*(n.)* a person who is ruled by another; a topic or course of study.

87. **sultry**—*(adj.)* uncomfortably hot and close; very hot and humid.

88. **synopsis**—*(n.)* a brief or condensed summary.

89. **tarnish**—*(v.)* to dull or discolor.

90. **tributary**—*(n.)* a small stream that flows into a larger stream.

91. **trinket**—*(n.)* a small object like jewelry, usually of little value.

92. **tumult**—*(n.)* noise; uproar; violent disturbance or disorder.

93. **turmoil**—*(n.)* commotion or disturbance.

94. **undaunted**—*(adj.)* not discouraged; undismayed.

95. **vagabond**—*(adj.)* wandering, homeless.—*(n.)* a wanderer.

96. **validate**—*(v.)* to make something legal or officially acceptable.

97. **vigilant**—*(adj.)* keenly attentive; alert.

98. **visionary**—*(adj.)* not practical; dreamy.—*(n.)* a person who is not practical; a dreamer.

99. **wick**—*(n.)* the part of a candle that is lighted.

100. **wrath**—*(n.)* strong, stern, fierce anger; punishment.